The Prisoner of Zenda

ANTHONY HOPE

Level 5

Retold by George F. Wear
Series Editors: Andy Hopkins and Jocelyn Potter

Library Learning Information

Idea Store® Bow
1 Gladstone Place
Roman Road
London E3 5ES

020 7364 4332

Created and managed by
Tower Hamlets Council

Pearson Education Limited
Edinburgh Gate, Harlow,
Essex CM20 2JE, England
and Associated Companies throughout the world.

ISBN 0 582 419360

First published in the Longman Simplified English Series 1939
First published in the Longman Fiction Series 1993
This adaptation first published 1996
Third impression 1997
This edition first published 1999

5 7 9 10 8 6 4

NEW EDITION

Copyright by John Hope-Hawkins
This edition copyright © Penguin Books Ltd 1999
Cover design by Bender Richardson White

Set in 11/14pt Bembo
Printed in Spain by Mateu Cromo, S.A.Pinto (Madrid)

Published by Pearson Education Limited in association with
Penguin Books Ltd, both companies being subsidiaries of Pearson Plc

For a complete list of the titles available in the Penguin Readers series please write to your local
Pearson Education office or to: Marketing Department, Penguin Longman Publishing,
80 Strand, London, WC2R 0RL

Contents

Introduction

In the second half of the nineteenth century, adventure stories set in strange countries were very popular with British readers. Anthony Hope was one of a group of writers that also included Robert Louis Stevenson, Arthur Conan Doyle and Rudyard Kipling, who became well known for stories of this kind. *The Prisoner of Zenda* is one of the very best adventure books from this period; it first appeared in 1894, and it has remained popular ever since then.

Anthony Hope is the pen name of Anthony Hope Hawkins, born in London in 1863, the son of a church minister. After leaving Oxford University in 1885 with a first-class degree, he practised law in London. Although a successful lawyer, he always wanted to write. After producing a number of short stories and paying for his first book to be printed, he was able to give up his work as a lawyer and turn to writing full time. He married in 1903, and had two sons and a daughter. During World War I he worked at the Ministry of Information, and in 1918 he was given a title in recognition of his war work. He died in 1933.

Hope's first book was *A Man of Mark* (1890). His first success, though, came when he wrote stories that made fun of fashionable London life for *The Westminster Gazette*. These appeared in book form a year later, under the title *The Dolly Dialogues* (1894), and were much enjoyed by readers at the time, although they are of less interest today. It was *The Prisoner of Zenda* that earned Hope great popularity and persuaded him to start writing full time. In 1898 he followed T*he Prisoner of Zenda* with a second book about one of the main characters, *Rupert of Hentzau*, which was almost as successful.

Hope wrote plays and popular stories, including *The Chronicles of Count Antonio* (1895), *Phroso* (1897), *Simon Dale* (1898) and

Sophy of Kravonia (1906). In 1900 he produced a more serious work of fiction, *Quisante*, about the life of a clever but unpleasant politician. Many of the stories are so imaginative that they are hardly believable. For example, *Sophy of Kravonia* tells of an English servant who finally becomes Queen of the Balkan state of Kravonia and attacks those who are responsible for the death of her royal husband. The main events are certainly improbable, but the detail in the description of the imaginary setting provided ideas for other writers. Hope actually wrote over thirty works of fiction, but none of the other books achieved quite the same success as *The Prisoner of Zenda*. He also wrote the story of his own life in a book called *Memories and Notes* (1927).

The setting for *The Prisoner of Zenda* is Ruritania, a country somewhere in central Europe invented by Hope. Hope's Ruritania is a country of castles, ancient towns, woods and mountains; a land of lords and servants, where honour and loyalty are important above all else. The book presented a romantic picture of central Europe for British and American readers of the time, and the word 'Ruritania' soon entered the English language to mean any mysterious, romantic country where adventures might happen.

The book was written in four weeks during 1893 and appeared in 1894. It was an immediate success, earning high praise from other writers. It was turned into a play and was equally popular on the stage. The story was perfectly suited to the new film industry, and has been made into a film at least four times, featuring some great stars of the screen. One reason for the popularity of the two books about Ruritania was that they were shorter and more exciting than many works of fiction of the time. The story contains all the features of a good adventure: chance, surprise, danger, skill and love. The main character, Rudolf Rassendyll, is a courageous, active man who tells of his adventures with a humour that is immediately attractive to the reader. The most interesting of the other characters is the daring Rupert Hentzau, who wins Rudolf's respect with his cool nerve, even though his mind and acts are evil.

The book opens with adventure-loving young Rudolf Rassendyll at home in England, looking for excitement. He has very few responsibilities in the world and time to fill. He has travelled widely and speaks a number of European languages extremely well. He reads in the papers that a new king, Rudolf the Fifth, is going to be crowned in Ruritania. It will be a grand occasion of great ceremony, and he decides to go there.

When he arrives in the country, he goes to stay in the town of Zenda. Walking in the forest, he meets the new King and discovers that he looks just like him; their most unusual common feature is their red hair. The King finds the similarity between them very amusing at first, but it becomes important as young Rudolf becomes involved in the King's problems. He finds himself the enemy of the evil duke, Black Michael, and Michael's loyal but cruel men, the 'famous Six'. Rudolf also has to decide how to behave with the beautiful Princess Flavia, who believes him to be King, when he finds – in spite of himself – that he is falling in love with her. Rudolf needs all the quick thinking and courage he was born with to escape from the dangerous game he finds himself playing in this faraway country.

Chapter 1   The Rassendylls

'When in the world are you going to *do* anything, Rudolf?' asked my brother's wife one morning at breakfast.

'My dear Rose,' I answered, 'why should I do anything? My position is a comfortable one. I have enough money – or nearly enough – for my needs (no one ever has quite enough you know); I enjoy a good social position. I am brother to Lord Burlesdon and, through him, to that lovely lady, his wife. Surely it is enough!'

'You are twenty-nine,' she remarked, 'and you've done nothing but—'

'Travel? It is true. Our family doesn't need to do things.'

This remark of mine rather annoyed Rose, for everyone knows that, pretty as she is herself, her family is hardly of the same rank as the Rassendylls. Besides her attractions she possessed a large fortune, and my brother Robert, Lord Burlesdon, was wise enough not to mind whether her family were ancient or not.

Well, if my life had been a useless one in Rose's eyes, I had enjoyed a good deal of pleasure and picked up a good deal of knowledge. I had been to a German school and a German university, and spoke German as perfectly as I spoke English. I was also quite good at French. I was, I believe, a fairly good swordsman, and a good shot. I could ride any kind of a horse, and I was as calm and sensible as any man, in spite of the flaming red hair on my head.

'The difference between you and Robert,' said Rose, 'is that he recognizes the duties of his position, and you only see the opportunities of yours.'

'To a man of spirit, my dear Rose,' I answered, 'opportunities are duties.'

1

'Nonsense!' said she, throwing her head back, and after a moment she went on: 'Now here is Sir Jacob Borrodaile offering you exactly what you need.'

'A thousand thanks!' I put in.

'He's to be an ambassador in six months, and Robert says that he'll take you with him to work for him. Do take the position, Rudolf – to please me.'

Now, when Rose puts the matter in that way, resting those pretty little eyes on me with such an anxious look, twisting her little hands, all because of a lazy person like myself, for whom she has no natural responsibility, the voice of conscience wakes in me. Besides, I thought it possible I could pass the time in the position suggested with some amusement. Therefore I said: 'My dear Rose, if in six months' time nothing has happened to prevent me, and Sir Jacob invites me, well, then, I'll go with him.'

'Oh, Rudolf, how good of you! I *am* glad!'

And so my promise was given; but six months is a long time, and I wanted to find something interesting to do in that period. It suddenly came to my mind that I would visit Ruritania, as I saw in the papers that Rudolf the Fifth was to be crowned at Strelsau in the course of the next three weeks, with great ceremony.

For various reasons I had never been to that highly interesting and important kingdom, which, though a small one, had played no small part in European history, and might do the same again under the power of a young and strong ruler, such as the new king was said to be. I made up my mind to go, and began my preparations.

It has never been my practice to tell my relations where I am going on my many journeys, and as I did not want to be opposed in this case, I simply said I was going for a walking tour in the Alps. Rose was not very pleased, but when I suggested I might write a book about the political and social problems of the area, she cried out with pleasure.

'That would be lovely,' she said, 'wouldn't it, Robert?'

'It is one of the best ways of introducing yourself to political life these days,' said Robert, who had written several books himself.

'Now promise you'll do it,' said Rose earnestly.

'No, I won't promise, but if I find enough material, I will.'

'That's fair enough,' said Robert.

'Oh, material doesn't matter,' said Rose.

But she could not get more than a half-promise out of me. To tell the truth, I did not think for a moment that the story of my tour that summer would mark any paper or spoil any pen. And that shows how little we know what the future holds. For here I am, carrying out my half-promise, and writing, as I never thought to write, a book – though it will hardly serve as an introduction to political life, and it has nothing to do with the Alps. Nor would it please Rose, I fear, if I ever gave it her to read, but that is something which I have no intention of doing.

◆

On my way through Paris, a friend came to see me at the station. As we stood talking by the train, he suddenly left me to speak to a lady. Following him with my eyes, I saw him raise his hat to a graceful and fashionably dressed woman, about thirty, tall and dark. In a moment or two he returned to me.

'You've got a lovely travelling companion,' my friend told me. 'That's Antoinette de Mauban, and they say that the Duke of Strelsau – King Rudolf's brother you know – has paid her his attentions. She is a widow, rich and hoping to improve her situation. Who knows what she is aiming for?'

But the pretty widow did not appear to want to know me; I saw no more of her, although we were on the same train.

As soon as I reached the Ruritanian border (where the official looked at me as if he had seen a ghost), I bought the papers, and found in them news which would have an effect on my movements. For some unexplained reason the date of the coronation had been suddenly brought forward, and was to take place in two days' time. The whole country was excited about it, and I learnt that Strelsau was crowded. Rooms were all booked and hotels overflowing; there would be very little chance of my getting a room without paying a very high price.

So I decided to stop at Zenda, a small town fifty miles from the capital and about ten from the border. My train reached there in the evening; I would spend the next day, Tuesday, walking over the hills, and taking a look at the famous castle, and go by train to Strelsau on the Wednesday morning, returning at night to sleep at Zenda.

I therefore got out at Zenda, and as the train passed where I stood, I saw Madame de Mauban in her place; clearly she was going through to Strelsau, having, with more thought than I, booked a room there.

I was very kindly received at the small hotel, which was kept by a rather large old lady and her two daughters. They were good, quiet people. The old lady was fond of the Duke, who was now master of the Zenda lands and of the castle, which rose grandly on a steep hill at the end of the valley, a mile or so from the hotel. The old lady was in fact sorry that the Duke was not on the throne, instead of his brother.

'We know Duke Michael,' said she. 'He has always lived among us; every Ruritanian knows Duke Michael. But the King is almost a stranger; he has been abroad, and not one person in ten knows him even by sight.'

'And now,' said one of the young women, 'they say he has shaved off his beard, so that no one at all knows him.'

'Shaved his beard!' cried her mother. 'Who says so?'

'Johann, the Duke's forest guard. He has seen the King.'

4

'Ah, yes. The King, sir, is now at the Duke's hunting lodge in the forest here; from here he goes to Strelsau to be crowned on Wednesday morning.'

I was interested to hear this, and made up my mind next day to walk in the direction of the lodge, on the chance of seeing the King.

'I wish he would stay at his hunting lodge,' went on the old woman, 'and let our Duke be crowned on Wednesday.'

'As for me,' said the younger and prettier of the two daughters, 'I hate Black Michael! A red Elphberg for me, mother! The King's hair, they say, is as red as – as – '

She laughed as she looked across at me.

'Many a man has hated his red hair before now,' said the old lady.

'But never a woman!' cried the girl.

I thought it time to prevent a quarrel. 'Why is the King here?' I asked. 'It is the Duke's land, you say.'

'The Duke invited him, sir, to rest here until Wednesday. The Duke himself is at Strelsau, preparing to receive the King.'

'Then they're friends?'

The younger girl threw back her head, 'Yes,' she said, 'they love one another as men do who want the same place and the same wife!'

The old woman looked angry, so I said quickly: 'The same place? You mean the throne, I suppose. But the same wife? How's that, young lady?'

'All the world knows that Black Michael – well, then, mother, the Duke – would give his soul to marry his cousin, the Princess Flavia, who is to be the Queen.'

'Well,' I said, 'I begin to be sorry for your Duke. But a younger son has to take what the older one leaves, and be as thankful to God as he can.' I laughed, thinking of Madame de Mauban and her journey to Strelsau.

A heavy step sounded at the door and a man came in.

'We have company, Johann,' said my hostess, and the man pulled off his cap.

The moment he looked at me, to my surprise he took a step back as though, like the border official, he had seen something surprising.

'What's the matter, Johann?' asked the older girl. 'This is a gentleman on his travels, come to see the coronation.'

The man had calmed himself, but he was looking at me in a strange, almost fierce, manner.

'Good evening to you,' said I.

'Good evening, sir,' he replied in a low voice, and the younger girl began to laugh.

'See, Johann,' she said, 'it is the colour you love. He was surprised at your hair, sir. It's not the colour we see most of, here in Zenda.'

'I beg your pardon, sir,' said Johann.

I then said good night to them all and rose to my feet. The young girl ran to light the way to my room. Johann still looked at me strangely as I passed. While the girl was leading me up the stairs, she said: 'Master Johann could never be pleased with one of your colouring, sir.'

'Perhaps he prefers yours,' I suggested.

'I meant, sir, in a man.'

'What,' I asked, 'does hair colour matter in a man?'

'I don't know, sir, but I like yours – it's the Elphberg red.'

'Colour in a man,' said I, 'is a matter of no more importance than that!' – and I gave her something of no value.

'I hope the kitchen door is shut,' she said.

'Let's hope so,' I answered, and left her.

In fact, though, as I now know, hair colour is sometimes of great importance to a man.

Chapter 2   A Merry Evening with a New Relation

The next day I discovered that by walking ten miles through the forest, I could come to the railway again at a small station. So having said goodbye to my kind friends, I set out to climb the hill that led to the castle, and from there to the forest of Zenda. The oldest part of the castle was still in a good state of preservation. Round it was a moat, deep and broad, and on the other side a fine modern building put up by the last King. It was now the country house of the Duke of Strelsau.

When I came nearer, I saw that the old and the new parts were joined by a drawbridge; in fact that was the only way into the old castle. A broad driveway led to the new building. I thought how convenient for Duke Michael this was; if he wanted to see no one, he could cross the bridge, and have it pulled in after him (it ran on rollers). Nothing less than a company of soldiers with heavy guns could get him out.

Passing on, I soon entered the forest and walked for an hour or more in its cool shade. It was a lovely place, the great trees touching each other over my head, the sunshine sliding through here and there. After a time I sat down by a fallen tree trunk to smoke my pipe and enjoy myself in peace. When it was finished I went off into a very pleasant sleep, in spite of the fact that I was on the private property of Duke Michael. I was woken by a voice, rough and loud.

'What the devil have we got here! Shave him, and he'd be the King!'

I opened my eyes, and found two men looking at me with much curiosity. Both wore shooting dress and carried guns. One was rather short and very strongly built, with a big square head, a grey moustache and small light blue eyes. The other was a thin young man of middle height, with dark hair, rather graceful. I understood the first to be a soldier, the second a gentleman used

7

to moving in good society, but with something of the army about him too. It appeared afterwards that my guess was a good one.

The older one came up to me, followed by the other, who politely raised his hat. I rose slowly to my feet.

'He's the right height, too,' said the older man, in a low voice, looking at my six feet two inches. Then, with a careless touch of his hat, he said: 'May I ask your name?'

'As you have taken the first step, gentlemen,' said I, with a smile, 'suppose you tell me yours first.'

The young man smiled pleasantly. 'This,' said he, 'is Colonel Sapt, and I am called Fritz von Tarlenheim. We are both in the service of the King of Ruritania.'

I bowed and, taking off my hat, answered: 'I am Rudolf Rassendyll, a traveller from England. Once for two or three years I was an officer in the army of Her Majesty Queen Victoria.'

'Then we are all brothers of the sword,' answered Tarlenheim, holding out his hand, which I took immediately.

'Well, Mr Rassendyll,' said Sapt in his deep voice, 'you may not know it, but you look exactly like our King.'

This made me feel uncomfortable, and I remembered the looks of the official and of Johann the day before. If I had known this, I would have given more thought to my visit to Ruritania. But it was too late now.

At this moment a ringing voice sounded from the wood behind us.

'Fritz, Fritz! Where are you, man?'

Tarlenheim turned, and said quickly: 'It's the King!'

Old Sapt laughed as a young man jumped out from behind the trunk of a tree and stood beside us. As I looked at him, I gave a cry of surprise, and he, seeing me, stepped back in equal surprise. Except for the hair on my face and a consciousness of rank which his position gave him, the King of Ruritania might have been

Rudolf Rassendyll, and I, Rudolf Rassendyll, the King.

The King found his voice first.

'Colonel – Fritz – who is this gentleman?'

'It seems that you have a double, sire,' said Sapt drily.

His surprise over, the King looked at me again, and then burst out laughing.

'Well met, brother!' he cried, stepping up to me and taking my hand. 'You must forgive my surprise. Tell me who you are, and where you are going.'

I did so, but he seemed to look doubtful when I said I was going to Strelsau the next day. Then he laughed again.

'Fritz, Fritz,' he cried. 'I'd give a thousand pounds to see Brother Michael's face when he sees a pair of us!'

'Seriously, sire,' remarked Fritz, 'I do not think it would be wise for Mr Rassendyll to visit Strelsau just now.'

The King lit a cigarette. 'Well, Sapt?' he said.

'He mustn't go,' said the old man roughly.

'You mean, Colonel, that I should be in Mr Rassendyll's debt if—'

'Enough, sire,' said I. 'I leave Ruritania tonight.'

'No, you certainly don't,' replied the King. 'And that is spoken directly, as Sapt likes it. You will have dinner with me tonight, whatever happens afterwards. Come, man, you don't meet a new brother every day.'

Sapt and Fritz agreed, so we set off walking through the forest. The King smoked cigarette after cigarette and talked without pause. He was a merry and interesting companion. Coming out of the wood after about half an hour, we found ourselves in front of a small, roughly built hunting lodge. It had a single floor, and was made of wood. A servant came out to meet us, and I also saw a fat old woman, who, I learned later, was the mother of Johann, the forest guard.

'Well, is dinner ready, Josef?' asked the King.

'Yes, Your Majesty,' the servant answered, and soon we sat down to a plentiful meal. The King called for wine.

'Remember tomorrow,' said Fritz. 'We have to make an early start.'

'Yes – tomorrow!' laughed old Sapt.

The King drank my health, calling me 'his new brother', and I replied with 'Long life to the Elphbergs!'

The food was plain enough, but the wine was beyond all price or praise, and we did it justice. Fritz's attempts to stop the King were hopeless. In fact, he was soon easily persuaded to go on drinking himself, and it wasn't very long before we were all more full of wine than we ought to have been. The King talked of what he would do in the future, Old Sapt talked of what he had done in the past, and Fritz of some beautiful girl or other, and I of the greatness of Ruritania. We all talked at once, and – tomorrow was forgotten.

At last the King sat back in his chair and said he had drunk enough. Josef then set in front of us a grand old bottle.

'The Duke of Strelsau told me to set this wine in front of the King when the King was tired of all other wines,' he said.

'Well done, brother Michael!' cried the King. 'Open it, Josef! It's the very last one.'

The King lifted his glass and tasted the wine. Then he turned to us.

'Gentlemen, my friends, Rudolf, my brother, everything that I have is yours too, and that includes half of Ruritania. But don't ask me for a single drop of this most excellent bottle. I drink to the health of that – that devil, Black Michael.'

And the King seized the bottle, turned it over his mouth, and drank it to the last drop. Then he threw the bottle against the wall. The sound of the breaking glass was the last thing I heard for many, many hours. We all fell asleep where we were.

I woke suddenly, wet from head to foot, to see Old Sapt with a bucket in his hand. By him was Fritz, sitting on the table and looking as pale as a ghost. I jumped to my feet in anger.

'Your joke goes too far,' I cried, rubbing the water from my eyes and hair.

'There's no time to quarrel,' returned Sapt. 'Nothing else would wake you. It's five o'clock.'

'And what's that to me?' I demanded hotly.

'Rassendyll,' interrupted Fritz, getting down from the table and taking my arm, 'look here.'

The King lay full length on the floor. His face was as red as his hair, and he breathed heavily. Sapt disrespectfully kicked him sharply, but he made no movement. I saw that his face and head were wet with water, as were mine.

'We've spent half an hour on him,' said Fritz.

I knelt down and felt his heartbeat; it seemed terribly slow.

'That last bottle must have been drugged,' I suggested. 'We must get a doctor.'

'There's none within ten miles, and a thousand doctors wouldn't get him to Strelsau today,' answered Sapt.

'But the coronation?' I cried.

'We shall have to send word that he's ill,' said Fritz.

Old Sapt laughed scornfully. 'If he's not crowned today, he never will be.'

'But why?' I asked.

'The whole nation is there to meet him; half the army with Black Michael at its head. Shall we send word that the King's too drunk to come?'

'That he's ill,' I corrected.

'Ill!' repeated Sapt with another scornful laugh. 'The people know his illnesses too well. He's been "ill" before.'

'We must take a risk on what they think,' said Fritz.

'You say,' Sapt said to me, 'you think the King was drugged?'

'Certainly.'

11

'Then who drugged him? Why, Black Michael, of course. His reason? To prevent him from coming to be crowned. You know,' he continued, turning to Fritz, 'that half Strelsau would prefer Michael as king. I tell you, that if Rudolf the Fifth is not crowned today, Michael the First will take his place.'

For a moment or two we were all silent; then Sapt turned to me and said, 'As a man grows old he believes more and more in chance. Chance sent you here. Chance sends you now to Strelsau.'

I jumped up, shouting, 'You don't mean . . . Good God!'

Fritz looked up, a sudden eager look on his face.

'Impossible!' I answered. 'I would be known.'

'It's a risk,' said Sapt, 'but on the other side it's a certainty. You won't be known if you shave. Are you afraid?'

'Certainly not!'

'Come, my boy, forgive me. But it will cost you your life, you know, if you're discovered – and mine, and Fritz's here. If you don't go, I swear to you that Black Michael will sit tonight on the throne, and the King will lie in prison or his grave.'

'The King would never forgive us,' I said.

'Are we women? Who cares for his forgiveness?'

The seconds passed – fifty, sixty, seventy . . . and then I suppose a look came over my face, for Old Sapt caught me by the hand, crying: 'You'll go?'

'Yes, I'll go,' I said, looking at the figure of the King lying there on the floor.

Chapter 3   The King Keeps His Appointment

The next two hours passed like a dream. It was fortunate that Sapt was there to think for me, and for Fritz too. Old Sapt thought of everything. He called in Josef and made him shave me. The King

12

was carried into the wine cellar down below. As for the fat woman, Johann's mother, Sapt thought she might have been listening to our plans from the other side of the door, so he tied her up and put a cloth in her mouth, and locked her in another of the cellar rooms.

'The guard!' cried Fritz. 'What will happen? They'll know.'

'Michael is sending a guard to go with the King,' Sapt explained to me. 'We'll go without them, take the train at Hofbau instead of Zenda, and when they come, the bird will have flown.'

'If they know anything of Michael's plans,' said I, 'they'll only think we too had an idea of them.'

I then put on the King's white uniform, and Sapt and Fritz also put on theirs. Josef was left with strict orders to guard the cellar until we returned. We jumped on our horses – the King's horses – and rode off through the forest.

On the way Sapt explained as much as he could of the King's past life, his family, his likes and dislikes, his friends, companions and servants. He told me the rules of the Ruritanian Court, and promised to be at my side at every moment of the day. Fritz spoke little, riding like a man in a dream.

We were by now at the station. Fritz had calmed down enough to explain to the surprised stationmaster the King's change of plans. The train arrived; we were just in time. As soon as we were safely in a first-class carriage, Sapt went on with his lessons. I looked at my watch – the King's watch, of course – and saw it was just after eight.

'Perhaps they've gone to look for us,' I said, thinking anxiously of what might be happening at the lodge.

'No use thinking now,' said Sapt. 'For today you've got to think of nothing but the fact that you're the King.'

At half past nine, looking out of the window, I saw the towers and houses of a great city.

'Your capital, Your Majesty,' laughed Sapt with a wave of his hand and, leaning forward he felt my heartbeat. 'A little too quick,' he said.

'I'm not made of stone!' I cried.

'All right, you'll do,' he answered. 'As for you, Fritz, we must say you've caught a cold. You are shaking like a leaf.'

'We're an hour earlier than they expected,' said Sapt. 'I'll have word sent of your arrival. For now, though—'

'For now,' said I, 'the King wants some breakfast.'

Old Sapt laughed. 'Spoken like an Elphberg,' he said.

The train stopped. Fritz and Sapt jumped out, took off their hats and held the door for me. I tried to swallow a lump that had risen in my throat, put my hat firmly on my head, then stepped out of the train.

A moment later, all was hurry and confusion; men running up, and then away again; men leading me to the restaurant; men getting on horses and riding at great speed in various directions. While I was still swallowing the last drop of my cup of coffee, the bells of the city began ringing, and the sound of a band and loud shouting came to my ears.

King Rudolf the Fifth was in his city of Strelsau! And I heard the people crying: 'God save the King!'

Sapt smiled. 'God save them both,' he whispered. 'Courage, my friend.'

As I stepped out of the restaurant, with Fritz and Sapt close behind me, a group of officers and people of high rank stood waiting for me. At their head was a tall old man in uniform.

'Marshal Strakencz,' whispered Sapt, and I knew that I was in the presence of the chief of the Ruritanian Army.

Just behind him was a short figure in long flowing clothes.

'The Chancellor,' whispered Sapt. So this was my chief minister.

The Marshal greeted me with a few loyal words, and gave a short explanation of the absence of the Duke of Strelsau. The

Duke, it seemed, had suddenly felt ill and could not come to the station. He asked for permission to wait for me at the church. I replied that I was sorry to hear of his illness. Several other people then came forward and, as no one showed any doubts about me, I began to feel some confidence. Fritz, though, was still pale, and his hand shook as he held it out to the Marshal.

Then we formed a procession and went to the station entrance. Here I climbed on my horse and set out, the Marshal on my right, Sapt on my left. The various officials went to their carriages and followed.

The city of Strelsau is partly old and partly new. Wide modern avenues and fine houses surround the narrow, twisting streets of the old town. In the outer circles live the upper classes; in the inner circles are the shops. Behind their rich fronts lie dirty narrow streets crowded with poor, disloyal, and often criminal classes. These social and local divisions marked, as I knew from Sapt's information, another division more important to me. The New Town was for the King; but the Old Town preferred Michael of Strelsau, and was not afraid to show it.

The scene was a grand one as we passed along the main street to the square where the royal palace stood. Here I was in the middle of my own people, every house covered with flags. All along the way, on both sides, the crowds cheered and waved. I almost began to feel that I really was the King, until suddenly by chance I raised my eye to a window and there saw Antoinette de Mauban, the woman who had travelled with me from Paris.

I saw her lean forward and look at me. I found myself feeling for my revolver. Suppose she had cried, 'That's not the King!'

Well, we rode on, and in a few minutes the Marshal gave an order, and the guards on horseback closed round me. We were entering the poorer area loyal to Duke Michael. This action showed more clearly than the words of Sapt the state of feeling in the town.

'Why this change in our order, Marshal?' I asked.

The Marshal bit his white moustache. 'It is safer, sire,' he said in a low voice.

I stopped my horse. 'Let those in front ride on,' said I, 'until they are fifty yards ahead. You, Marshal, and Colonel Sapt and my friends, wait here until I have ridden fifty yards. I will have the people see that their King trusts them.'

Sapt laid his hand on my arm. I shook him off. The Marshal looked uncertain.

'Am I not understood?' I said, and the Marshal, biting his moustache again, gave the orders. I saw Old Sapt smiling into his beard, and he shook his head at me. If I had been killed in the light of day in the streets of Strelsau, Sapt's position would have been a difficult one.

It was more interesting riding alone like that, because I heard the remarks of the crowds. At first there was a low sound from them, then a cheer; I am not ashamed to say that in my white uniform I was a good-looking figure. I heard several people say pleasant things about me, but the greater part remained silent, and my dear brother's picture was to be seen in most of the windows.

At last we were at the church. It was then that the full sense of what I was doing became clear to me. I got off my horse as in a dream, for it all seemed unreal. I marched into the fine ancient building with unseeing eyes, and noticed little of the well-dressed crowds waiting for me. I saw only two faces clearly, one that of a girl, pale and lovely, with hair of beautiful Elphberg red (for in a woman it is beautiful), the other that of a man with deep dark eyes and black hair. I knew this was Black Michael. He looked at me as if I was a ghost.

I remember almost nothing of the ceremony, except where taking the crown from the priest and putting it on my head. Then a man cried out, 'The Princess Flavia!' She bowed low to me and kissed my hand. Before I knew what to do, the priest was in front of me. Then came Black Michael, and I saw Sapt smiling into his beard again. My loving brother was shaking uncontrollably. But not in his face, nor in the Princess's, nor in anyone's, did I see the least doubt that I was the King.

Then back we went through the streets to the palace. I was in a carriage now, side by side with the Princess Flavia, and a rough man cried out: 'When's the marriage?' As he spoke another struck him in the face, shouting, 'Long live Duke Michael!' The Princess reddened and looked straight in front of her.

Now I felt uncomfortable, because I had forgotten to ask Sapt the state of my feelings, and how far matters had gone between the Princess and myself, or rather, the King. So I kept silent, but after a moment or two the Princess turned to me.

'Do you know, Rudolf,' said she, 'you look somehow different today?'

The fact was not surprising, but I felt worried.

'You seem much more earnest,' she went on, 'and I believe you're thinner. Is it possible that you have begun to take life seriously at last?'

I had to answer something, so I whispered softly, 'Would that please you?'

'Oh, you know my opinions,' she answered, looking away from me.

'Whatever pleases you I try to do,' I said, and as I saw her smile, and even turn red again, I thought I was playing the King's part for him very well. So I continued, and what I said was perfectly true: 'My dear cousin, nothing in my life has had more effect on me than the events of today.'

She smiled again, then became serious as she whispered: 'Did you notice Michael?'

'Yes. He wasn't enjoying himself, was he?'

'Do be careful!' she went on. 'You must keep a better watch on him, you know.'

'I know one thing,' I said; 'he wants what I've got.' Then I added, without any right to say such a thing for the King: 'And he also wants something which I haven't got yet, but hope to win some day.'

If I had been the King I would have thought her answer encouraging. She whispered, 'Haven't you enough responsibilities for one day, cousin?'

Bang! Bang! Bang!

We were at the palace gate. Guns were firing a greeting. I handed the Princess from the carriage, and we all went up the wide steps. Rows of servants were waiting as we went into the large dining room. I sat down with the Princess on my right, my brother on my left. All the other important people also sat down. Sapt stood behind my chair. At the other end of the table I saw Fritz drink a glass of wine to the bottom.

I asked myself what the King of Ruritania was doing.

Chapter 4   The Secret of a Cellar

We were in the King's dressing room – Fritz von Tarlenheim, Colonel Sapt and I. I threw myself into a comfortable chair. Sapt lit his pipe. He did not praise me on my success, but his whole manner showed how satisfied he was. Fritz was a new man.

'What a day for you to remember!' he said. 'I wouldn't mind being King myself for twelve hours. But didn't Black Michael look blacker than ever when you and the Princess had so much to say to each other?'

'How beautiful she is!' I cried.

'Never mind the woman,' said Sapt. 'Are you ready to start?'

'Yes,' I answered with a deep breath.

It was five o'clock, and at twelve I would be no more than Rudolf Rassendyll. I remarked on it in a joking way.

'You'll be lucky if you *are* still Rudolf Rassendyll,' said Sapt. 'I feel my head shaking on my shoulders every moment you are in the city. Michael has had news from Zenda. He went into another room to read it, and came out looking angry.'

'I'm ready,' I said, this news making me all the more eager to go.

'Now, Fritz,' said Sapt, 'the King goes to bed. He is tired. No one is to see him until nine tomorrow morning. You understand – no one?'

'I understand, Colonel,' said Fritz.

'Not even Black Michael,' added Sapt. 'If the door of this room is opened while we're away, you're not to be alive to tell us about it.'

'I do not need teaching what my duty is,' said Fritz, a little annoyed.

Sapt and I wrapped ourselves up, I dressing as his servant. We then went through a secret door, along a dark passage and came out into a quiet road bordering on the palace garden. A man was waiting with two fine horses. Without a word we got on the horses and rode off.

There were some moments of danger as we passed the old city gate, but outside the city it was safe enough. It was a fine night and we rode hard, speaking little. We had done twenty-five miles when Sapt suddenly stopped.

'Listen!' he said.

Far behind us we heard the sound of horses' feet. The wind was blowing strongly towards us, and carried the sound easily.

'Come on!' said Sapt, and we made our horses go as fast as they could. The next time we stopped to listen, Sapt put his ear to the ground.

'There are two of them,' he said. 'You see where the road divides here? We go to the right, the other way leads to the castle. Each is about eight miles. Get down.'

'But they'll reach us,' I objected.

'Get down!' he repeated, and I obeyed. We had entered the forest of Zenda some time before, and the trees grew very thick here. We led our horses off the road, and waited in hiding.

'You want to see who they are?' I whispered.

'Yes, and where they are going.'

In a few moments the two riders were in sight. The moon was full, and we had a clear view.

'It's the Duke,' I said.

It was, and with him was a big strong man, whom I had reason to know well afterwards. He was Max Holf, brother of Johann, the forest guard. The two stopped at the fork in the road.

'Which way?' asked Black Michael.

'To the castle, sir.'

'Why shouldn't we go to the lodge?'

'I fear a trap. If all is well, why go to the lodge? If not, it's a trap to catch us.'

'All right, to the castle, then,' said the Duke, and in a moment the two horses were off up the road to the left.

We waited a few minutes.

'You see,' said Sapt, 'they've sent him a message that all is well.'

'What does that mean?'

'God knows,' answered Sapt, 'but it's brought him at great speed from Strelsau.'

Then we got on our horses and rode the last eight miles, our minds full of fear and surprise. 'All is well.' What did it mean?

At last the lodge came in sight. We rode up to the gate. All was still and quiet. No one came out to meet us. Then Sapt caught me by the arm. 'Look there,' he said.

I looked. At my feet were several pieces of torn and cut cloth.

'They're what I used to tie the old woman up with,' said Sapt.

We tied up our horses and hurried inside. Even Sapt had lost his usual calm. We ran down the steps to the cellar. The door stood wide open!

'They found the old woman,' I said.

'You might have known that from the cloths,' replied Sapt, 'but what of Josef? What of the King?'

Sapt was unable to enter the room. Afraid for himself he was not – no one could ever call him that – but he was afraid of what he might find in the dark cellar. I got a light and went in first. Over in the corner I saw the body of a man lying on his back, a red wound across his throat. All round him was blood that had flowed and was now dry.

I walked across and knelt down beside him. It was Josef. Sapt stood behind me, and he cried out in a strange voice: 'The King? My God, where is the King?'

I threw the lamp's light over every inch of the cellar.

'The King is not here,' I said.

It took Sapt ten minutes to calm himself. The clock in the dining room, where he had gone, struck one.

'They've got the King!' said Sapt in a hollow voice.

'Yes,' I answered. 'That explains Michael's message, "All's well". What a moment it was for him when he got it. It's hardly surprising he looked half crazy. I should like to know what he thought.'

'What does that matter? What does he think now?'

I rose to my feet.

'We must get back,' I cried, 'and collect every soldier in Strelsau. Michael will have to be caught.'

Old Sapt lit his pipe and made no move.

'The King may be murdered while we sit here,' I urged.

'That evil old woman,' said Sapt. 'She must have attracted their attention somehow. I see the game. They came here to take the King prisoner, thinking that he was drugged. If you hadn't gone to Strelsau, you and I and Fritz would have been murdered.'

'And the King?'

'Who knows where he is now?'

'Come, let us go,' I cried, and was surprised to see a strange smile light up the old man's face.

'Yes, we'll go,' he said. 'The King will be in his capital tomorrow.'

'The King?'

'The crowned King!'

'You're crazy!' I said.

'If we go back and tell them the trick we've played, what would you give for our lives?'

'Just what they're worth.'

'And the King's throne?' he went on. 'Do you think the lords and the people will enjoy being made fools of as they have been? Do you think they'll have a King who was too drunk to be crowned, and sent a servant to take his place?'

'The King was drugged – and I'm no servant,' I said, rather annoyed.

'I was giving you the story as Black Michael will tell it. My boy, if you play the man, you may save the King yet. Go back and keep his throne warm for him.'

'But the Duke will know by now; his servants will know.'

'Yes, but they can't speak!' he cried. 'How can they tell the truth about you without letting everyone know what they've done? Can they say, "This isn't the King, because we've taken the King prisoner and killed his servant"?'

I understood immediately. Whether Michael knew me or not, he could not speak. Unless he produced the King, what could he do? And if he did produce the King, what of his own hopes? But I also saw the difficulties.

'I will be discovered,' I argued.

'Perhaps, but every hour is something. Above all we must have a king in Strelsau, or the city will be Michael's in four-and-twenty hours, and what would the King's life be worth then, if he is still alive?'

'Yes, they may be killing him now. Sapt, suppose they do?'

'They won't, if you go to Strelsau. Do you think they'll kill him until you are out of the way? They would gain nothing by killing him to put you on the throne.'

It was a wilder and even more hopeless plan than the one we had carried out that day, but there seemed nothing else for me to do. Besides, I was young, and the danger attracted me.

'Sapt,' I cried, 'I'll try it!'

'Good. Now we must get away immediately.'

'We ought to bury poor Josef,' I said.

'No time – oh, all right, as you like. I'll get the horses; be quick.'

I carried the honest Josef up from the cellar, but met Sapt at the door. 'Put him down,' he said, 'someone is coming to do that for you.'

He took me to the window, and I saw 300 yards down the road to Zenda a party of eight horsemen. Some were carrying spades. No doubt they had been sent by Michael to remove all signs of their evil work. I pointed to the dead body on the floor.

'Colonel,' I said, 'we ought to strike a blow for him.'

'It's risky, Your Majesty, but – well, if we are killed, it'll save us a lot of thinking. I'll show you how we can attack them.'

We went through to the back door.

'Revolver ready?' asked Sapt.

'No, it's steel for me,' said I.

'Looking for a fight, eh?' said Sapt with a laugh. 'All right.'

We got on our horses, drawing our swords, and as soon as we heard the sound of the men at the front of the lodge, Sapt whispered, 'Now!'

We rushed as fast as we could round the house, and in a

moment were among them. Sapt told me later that he killed a man, and I believe him, but I saw no more of him. With a cut I broke open the head of someone on a brown horse, and he fell to the ground. A large man was opposite me, and there was another beside me. I rushed into the one in front and drove my sword into his breast as he fired a revolver. The bullet whistled past my ear. It was too dangerous to stay; I could not even pull out my sword, but left it in the man's body and went off at full speed after Sapt, whom I now saw twenty yards away. I waved my hand happily, but the next second dropped it with a cry as a bullet touched it and I felt the blood. In another moment or two we were out of sight.

Sapt laughed. 'Well, little Josef will have company,' he said. 'Did they notice you?'

'The large man did. As I struck him, I heard him cry, "The King!"'

'Good', said Sapt. Black Michael can expect more trouble from us yet.'

Chapter 5   A Fair Cousin and a Dark Brother

We reached the palace again without danger. Although it was after eight o'clock in the morning, we met very few people, and I was well wrapped up to hide my face. On entering the dressing room by the secret door, we saw Fritz lying fully dressed on a chair. He jumped up.

'Thank God, sire! Thank God you're safe,' he cried, and seized my hand to kiss it. Sapt, the cruel old man, laughed.

'That's good, my boy,' he said. 'We'll be all right.'

When Fritz understood, he fell back on the chair.

'Where's the King?' he cried.

'Quiet, you fool!' said Sapt. 'Not so loud! Here's the King.'

Then he added in a fierce whisper: 'Black Michael's got him –
alive, we think.'

After a pretence of having been to bed, I got up and had
breakfast. Then Sapt gave me a three-hour lesson on my duties. It
seemed to me that if a real king's life is a hard one, an acting king's
is much harder. Then came a visit from the Chancellor with all
kinds of papers to sign; my wounded finger came in very useful,
as it removed all doubts about my writing. I also had to meet
some of the ambassadors. It was a tiring day.

At last I was alone with Sapt and Fritz, and we had to decide
what was to be done.

'We ought to go and catch Black Michael at once,' said Fritz.

'Gently, gently,' urged Sapt. 'Would Michael fall and leave the
King alive?'

'Besides,' I said, 'how can the King for no clear reason suddenly
attack his dear brother Michael? The people would not accept
it.'

'Are we to do nothing, then?' said Fritz.

'We're to do nothing stupid,' replied Sapt roughly.

'It seems to me,' I said, 'that Michael and I are in the position
of two men each covering the other with a revolver, but as he has
the most to gain by doing something quickly, I must wait for him
to move.'

'Three of Michael's famous Six are in Strelsau,' said Fritz.

'Only three?' asked Sapt eagerly. 'Then the other three are at
Zenda, guarding the King. That means he is alive.'

Fritz's face brightened. 'Of course,' he said. 'If the King was
dead, all the Six would be here with Michael. He is back, you
know.'

'Gentlemen, gentlemen, who are the famous Six?' I asked.

'You'll soon meet them,' said Sapt. 'They are six gentlemen of
Michael's, and would do anything for him. There are three
Ruritanians, a Frenchman, a Belgian and an Englishman.'

'Any one of them would cut a throat if Michael ordered it,' said Fritz.

'Perhaps they'll cut mine,' I suggested.

'Nothing more likely,' said Sapt. 'Which of them are here, Fritz?'

'Bersonin, de Gautet and Detchard.'

'The foreigners! It's clear enough. The Ruritanians are guarding the King, so that they will be able to say nothing about Michael's game, being in it themselves.'

It was part of my plan to make myself as popular as I could, so I ordered my horse and went for a ride with Fritz in the fine park, then through some of the streets and, having in this way collected a crowd, I went to the house of the Princess Flavia. This caused much interest, and I heard shouts of approval. During my meeting with the Chancellor, he had suggested that the nation would be very happy to learn of a proposal of marriage, though of course he did not understand the difficulties in the way. The Princess was very popular, and I did not see that any harm could be done by paying her a visit, while it might help to improve the King's position. Fritz was surprisingly eager for such a visit. I discovered that he had a great desire to see the Princess's friend, the Countess Helga.

It was a difficult part for me to play. I had to show liking, but not feel it; keep the Princess attracted to me, but not be interested. It was made no easier by the fact that she was the most beautiful girl I had ever seen.

'I'm glad and proud, Rudolf,' she said, 'to see the change that has taken place in you. You are like the prince in Shakespeare who became a different man when he was king. Even your face has changed.'

This was a dangerous subject, so I chose another.

'My brother is back, I hear. He made a journey, it seems.'

'Yes, he is here,' she said, not looking pleased.

'Well, we are all glad to see him. The nearer he is, the better.'

The Princess smiled. 'You mean, cousin . . .?'

'That we can see better what he is doing? Perhaps. And why are you glad?'

'I never said that I was glad. I don't care in the least what Duke Michael is doing.'

If I had been the King, I should have felt encouraged. Just then there was a cheer from the street, and the Princess ran to the window.

'It is he!' she cried. 'It is the Duke himself!'

I smiled but said nothing. I heard the sound of feet in the outside room. I began to talk of general subjects. This went on for some minutes. Michael did not appear, but it did not seem to be for me to ask where he was. Suddenly, to my surprise, Flavia asked me in a troubled voice: 'Are you wise to make him angry?'

'What? Who? How am I making him angry?'

'By keeping him waiting, of course.'

'My dear cousin, I don't want to keep him waiting–'

'Well, then, he should come in?'

'Of course, if you wish it.'

She looked at me curiously. 'How funny you are,' she said. 'You know no one can come in without permission while you are here.'

Here was an interesting advantage in being a king! Inwardly I swore at Fritz for not telling me; I had nearly made a dangerous mistake. I jumped up, and went to the door, and brought Michael in.

'Brother,' I said, 'if I had known you were here, I would not have kept you waiting for a moment.'

He thanked me, but coldly. The man had many qualities, but he could not hide his feelings. Anyone could see that he hated me, and hated even more to see me with Princess Flavia. He knew I was not the King, but I believe he tried to hide from me what he knew.

'Your hand is hurt, sire,' he said.

'Yes,' I answered carelessly. 'I was playing a game with a dog, and it tried to bite me.'

He understood what I meant, and smiled bitterly.

'But there's no danger from the bite, is there?' asked Flavia anxiously.

'None from this,' I said. 'If I gave him a chance to bite more deeply, it would be different, cousin.'

'But surely the dog has been destroyed?' she continued.

'Not yet. We're waiting to see if his bite is harmful.'

'And if it is?' asked Michael.

'He'll be knocked on the head, brother,' I said. Then, remembering that I must seem to be friendly, I praised Michael for the arrangements he had made for the coronation, the state of the army and so on. Michael could not bear it. He rose suddenly to his feet.

'There are three friends of mine very anxious to be introduced to Your Majesty,' he said. 'They are here in the outer room.'

'Your friends are mine too, I hope,' I said politely, and walked with him to the door. He said goodbye to the Princess, and I took his arm. The look on his face gave me secret pleasure. As we entered the other room, Michael called his men.

He introduced them one by one, and they kissed my hand – de Gautet, a tall thin man with a big moustache; Bersonin the Belgian, rather fat, of middle height and completely without hair; and last, the Englishman, Detchard, a narrow-faced man, with close-cut fair hair and a sunburnt face. He looked a good fighter, but completely dishonest. I spoke to him in English, but as if I were a foreigner, and I believe he smiled, though he hid it at once.

'So Mr Detchard knows the secret,' thought I.

When they had gone, I returned to the Princess to say goodbye.

'Rudolf,' she said, very low, 'be careful, won't you?'

'Of what?'

'You know – I can't say. But think what your life is to . . .'

'Well, to . . .?'

'To Ruritania.'

Was I right to play the part, or wrong? I don't know, but I whispered softly: 'Only to Ruritania?'

She reddened. 'To your friends, too,' she said.

'Friends?'

'And to your cousin,' she whispered.

I could not speak. I kissed her hand and went out. Fritz was sitting next to the Countess Helga, careless of what the servants thought. He jumped up, and we left the house.

Chapter 6   A New Use for a Tea Table

Several days passed. My secret was still kept, though I had some bad moments and made some mistakes. I escaped discovery, though, and I think the reason was the daring of the plan. I believe it is easier to pretend to be a king successfully than to pretend to be one's next-door neighbour.

One day Sapt came into my room. He threw a letter on the table, saying, 'That's for you – a woman's writing, I think. But I've some news first. The King is in the Castle of Zenda.'

'How do you know?'

'Because the other half of Michael's Six are there. I've had inquiries made. They're all three there – Lauengram, Krafstein and Rupert Hentzau, three young devils, if ever there were any.'

'You think it's certain the King's there?'

'Yes. The drawbridge is kept pulled back, and no one is allowed in or out without an order from Michael or young Rupert.'

'I shall have to go to Zenda,' I said.

'Not yet, my boy. We've got to be careful. An open attack would mean the death of the King. What's in the letter?'

I opened it and read it aloud:

'If the King desires to know something very important for him, let him come alone to the house at the end of New Street at twelve o'clock tonight. The house is in a large garden, and there is a small gate in the wall at the back. If he opens the gate, turns to the right and walks twenty yards, he will find a summerhouse with six steps. Inside will be someone who will tell him something extremely important for his life and throne. This is written by a loyal friend. If he refuses this invitation, his life will be in danger, but he must come alone. Let him show this to no one, or he will ruin a woman who loves him; Black Michael does not forgive.'

'No,' remarked Sapt, as I ended, 'but he can write a very pretty letter.'

I thought the same, and was about to throw the letter away, when I saw there was some writing on the other side.

'If you are uncertain,' the writer continued, 'speak to Colonel Sapt—'

'Eh!' cried Sapt, in surprise. 'Does he take me for a greater fool than you?'

I continued:

'Ask him which woman would do most to prevent the Duke from marrying his cousin, and therefore most to prevent him from becoming King? Her name begins with A.'

I jumped to my feet, and Sapt laid down his pipe.

'Antoinette de Mauban!' I cried.

'How do you know?' he asked.

I told him what I knew of the lady. 'Yes,' he said thoughtfully, 'it's true that she's had a quarrel with Michael.'

'She could be useful to us, if she wished,' I remarked.

'I believe, though, that Michael wrote that letter.'

'So do I, but I intend to know for certain. I shall go, Sapt.'

'No, *I* shall go,' he replied.

'You may go as far as the gate,' I said.

'I shall go to the summerhouse.'

'Sapt,' I said, leaning back in my chair, 'I believe in that woman, and I shall go.'

'And I don't believe in any woman,' he replied, 'and you shan't go.'

'I either go to the summerhouse or back to England.'

Sapt had begun to learn how far he could lead or drive me, and when he must follow.

'All right,' he agreed.

To cut a long story short, at half past eleven that night Sapt and I got on our horses. Fritz was again left on guard. It was a dark night, and I carried a lamp, a knife and a revolver. We arrived outside the gate. I got off my horse.

'I shall wait here, then,' said Sapt. 'If I hear a shot I'll—'

'Stay where you are; it's the King's only chance. You mustn't be killed too.'

'You're right, my boy. Good luck!'

I went quietly through the gate into the garden. Turning to the right as the letter told me, I went slowly up the path, my lamp unlit, my revolver in my other hand. Soon I came to a large dark object — it was the summerhouse. I went silently up the steps, pushed open the door and walked in. A woman flew to me and seized my hand.

31

'Shut the door!' she whispered.

I did so, and turned the light of my lamp on her. It was Antoinette de Mauban, looking very beautiful, and dressed in fine clothes. The only furniture in the room was a chair or two and a small iron table such as one sees in coffee shops.

'Don't talk,' she said, 'there's no time. Listen! I know you, Mr Rassendyll. I wrote that letter at the Duke's orders.'

'So I thought,' said I.

'In twenty minutes three men will be here to kill you.'

'Three – the Three?'

'Yes. You must be gone by then. If not, you'll be killed.'

'Or they will.'

'Listen! When you're killed, your body will be taken to a low part of the town. It will be found there. Michael will immediately seize all your friends – Colonel Sapt and Fritz von Tarlenheim first. He will put the city under control of the army, and send a message to Zenda for the other Three to kill the King in the Castle. Then he'll make himself King and marry the Princess.'

'It's a pretty plan. But why, madam, do you–?'

'Give any reason you like – jealousy, if you wish. Now go; but remember, by night and day you are never safe. You have secret guards following you?'

'Yes,' I said. 'It's Sapt's idea.'

'Well, three men follow them. Michael's Three are never more than 200 yards from you. Now go – not by the gate; there will be a guard on it by now. There is a ladder against the wall on this side of the summerhouse. Climb over it, and fly for your life.'

'Madam,' said I, 'you have served the King well tonight, though it will mean danger for yourself. Where is he in the castle?'

She lowered her voice to a fearful whisper.

'Across the drawbridge you come to a heavy door; behind that lies – Listen! What's that?'

32

There were steps outside.

'They're coming! They're too soon! Put out your lamp!'

I did as she said, and then looked through a crack in the door. I could just see three figures. I pulled out my revolver. Antoinette quickly put her hand on my arm.

'You may kill one,' said she. 'But what then?'

A voice came from outside – speaking perfect English.

'Mr Rassendyll,' it said.

I made no answer.

'We want to talk to you. Will you promise not to shoot until we've done?'

'Have I the pleasure of speaking to Mr Detchard?'

'Never mind names.'

'Then let mine alone.'

'All right, sire. I've an offer for you.'

I still had my eye to the crack. The three had come up two more steps; their revolvers pointed full at the door.

'Will you let us in? On our honour, we shall not shoot.'

'Don't trust them,' whispered Antoinette.

'We can speak through the door,' I said.

'Will you promise not to open it and shoot?'

'I'll promise not to shoot before you do,' I answered, 'but I'll not let you in. Stand outside and talk.'

'That's sensible,' said Detchard.

Still looking through the crack, I saw they were now on the top step just outside the door.

'Don't trust them,' said Antoinette again, but I did not need her warning. I knew they meant to rush me as soon as I began to talk.

'Well, gentlemen,' I said, 'what's the offer?'

'A safe journey to the border, and fifty thousand English pounds.'

'That seems generous,' I replied. 'Give me a minute to consider.'

I turned to Antoinette, and whispered: 'Stand close up against the wall, out of the line of fire from the door.'

'What are you going to do?' she asked in fear.

'You'll see,' said I.

I picked up the iron tea table. It was not heavy for a man of my strength, and I held it by the legs. The top gave a complete protection to my head and body. I tied my lamp to my belt, and put my revolver in my pocket. Then I went to the back of the room and, holding the table in front of me, called out: 'All right, gentlemen, I accept your offer, depending on your honour. If you will open the door–'

'Open it yourself,' said Detchard.

'It opens outwards,' I said. 'Stand back a little, gentlemen.'

I pretended to try to open it, then slipped back to my place.

'It won't open properly,' I said. 'Pull it from that side.'

'I'll open it,' cried Detchard. 'What, Bersonin, are you afraid of one man?'

I smiled to myself. A moment later the door was thrown back, and the three stood there, their revolvers pointing straight at me. With a shout I charged them as hard as I could. Three shots rang out, but the table protected me. The next moment I was into them, or rather the table was, and all four of us were rolling together in a confused group down the steps. Antoinette de Mauban cried out, but I rose to my feet, laughing aloud.

De Gautet and Bersonin lay still. Detchard was under the table, but as I rose, he pushed it from him and fired again. I pulled out my revolver and fired back at him; I heard him swear. Then I ran like the wind past the summerhouse along the wall. The wall was high.

'Please God,' said I to myself, 'she told me the truth about the ladder!'

Yes, there it was. I was up and over in a minute. Running along the outside, I saw the horses, then Sapt. He was struggling with the lock of the now barred gate, and firing at it wildly. He had quite forgotten that he was not to take part in the fight.

'Come along,' I cried to him, laughing.

'You're safe? What are you laughing at?'

'Four gentlemen round a tea table,' I answered. It had certainly been uncommonly funny to see the famous and dangerous Three defeated by a weapon no more terrible than an ordinary tea table.

Besides, as you see, I had honourably kept my word, and I had not fired until they did.

Chapter 7   A Question of Honour

From secret police reports I learned the next day that Michael had left Strelsau, and the Three with him. Detchard, it appeared, had a wounded arm. I was glad to hear I had left my mark on the man. Antoinette de Mauban had also left. They could only be going to Zenda. What was more important to me was the following statement in one of the reports:

The King is much criticized for taking no steps about his marriage; it is believed that the Princess Flavia is also sad. Many people are mentioning her name together with that of the Duke of Strelsau.

The chief of police is told to speak quite openly,' said Sapt, when I made an angry sound.

'It is quite true about the Princess,' said Fritz. 'The Countess Helga told me that Flavia was already much in love with the King–'

'Enough!' I cried.

'I have ordered a grand dance to be held tonight at the royal palace in the Princess's honour,' said Sapt.

'That's news to me,' I said, not feeling at all pleased.

'The arrangements are all made,' said Fritz.

Sapt came up to me, and said in a sharp voice: 'You must offer her marriage when you speak to her tonight.'

'Good heavens!'

'I suppose,' said Sapt, 'you've made pretty speeches to a girl before now. That's all she wants.'

'I refuse,' I said. 'I won't share in any plan to make a fool of the Princess.'

Sapt looked at me with his small, clever eyes, and smiled.

'All right, my boy. We mustn't press you too far,' he said, 'but talk nicely to her. We can't allow her to get annoyed with the King.'

I went for a short walk in the garden with Fritz. I knew why Sapt gave up urging me to speak words of love. He knew himself that her beauty and my own feeling would carry me farther than all his arguments. He must have seen the unhappiness he was causing her, but that meant nothing to him. If the King was saved, she would have to marry him, either knowing or not knowing the change. If not – well, we had never spoken of it, but I believe that Sapt intended to keep me on the throne rather than let Black Michael get it.

The dance was a great affair. How could I remain cold and unfeeling beside such a beautiful woman, especially when her eyes met mine . . . In sight of all, I took from around my neck a chain from which the Red Rose of Ruritania hung, and I placed the chain over her head. Everyone cheered. I saw Sapt smiling, and Fritz looking annoyed.

When it was all over, I was alone with her in a little room looking over the garden. She was sitting, and I stood before her. I was struggling with myself, and if she had not looked at me, I believe even then I should have won my fight. But she gave me just one sudden look . . . and I was lost! I forgot the King in

Zenda. I forgot the King in Strelsau. She was a Princess – and I a deceiver. Do you think I remembered that? I threw myself on my knee before her and took her hands in mine. I said nothing. Why should I?

Then she pushed me away, crying suddenly, 'Ah, is it true? Or is it because you must?'

'It's true!' I said. 'It's true that I love you more than life – or truth – or honour!'

She understood no special meaning from my words, thinking them the wild sweet manner of love.

'How is it that I love you now, Rudolf?'

'Now?'

'Yes, just lately. I – I never did before.'

How joy filled me! It was I, Rudolf Rassendyll, that she loved. How sweet it tasted!

'You didn't love me before?'

She looked up into my face, and said smiling, 'It must have been your crown. I felt it first on Coronation Day.'

'Oh, Flavia, if I were not the King–'

'Whatever you were, I should love you just the same,' she said.

There was still a chance for me to save my honour.

'Flavia,' I began, in a strange dry voice that seemed not my own. 'I am not–'

There was a heavy step outside the window, and Sapt appeared. My half-finished sentence died on my lips. He looked at me disapprovingly and bowed.

'Sire, a thousand pardons, but a group of Lords have been waiting for a quarter of an hour to say goodbye.'

I met his eye directly; and I read in it an angry warning. How long he had been a listener, I don't know, but he had broken into the conversation just in time.

'I must not keep them waiting,' I said.

'Oh, Colonel Sapt,' cried Flavia, 'I am so happy!'

There was no mistaking her meaning, and I really believe some gentleness came into Sapt's voice as he kissed her hand and said, 'God save you, madam!' Then he stood up straight and added, 'But before all, comes the King!'

'Yes,' said Flavia. 'God save the King!'

I went into the dance room again to receive goodbyes. I saw Sapt going in and out of the crowd, and where he had been were smiles and whispers. I knew what he was doing, the old devil. He was spreading the news that he had learned. To save the Crown and beat Black Michael – that was his one aim. Such news spreads fast, and when I went out to the front gate to hand Princess Flavia into her carriage, there was a large crowd waiting for us. They welcomed us with thundering cheers. What could I do? By Sapt's tricks and my own uncontrolled feelings I had been forced on, and the way back was closed behind me.

Later – it was nearly daylight – I was alone with Sapt and Fritz.

'Sapt,' I said, 'you have left me no honour. Unless you want me to become a criminal as well, let us go to Zenda and crush Black Michael, and bring the King back.'

'If you tried–' he began.

'If I tried,' I interrupted, 'I could marry the Princess, and nothing you could do would be able to stop me. Do you think anyone would believe your story, if you told the truth?'

'I know,' he said quietly.

'Then are we going to Zenda?'

He took me by the hand. 'By God, you're the finest Elphberg of them all!' he cried 'But I am the King's servant. God save the King! Come, we'll go to Zenda.'

Plans were quickly made. I gave Marshal Strakencz orders as to what to do if the King was killed – he thought I meant myself of course, and was full of trouble at my words.

'May God preserve Your Majesty,' he said, 'for I think you are going on a dangerous journey.'

'I hope that no life more important than mine may be demanded,' I replied.

It was more difficult to tell Flavia that I was leaving her. Before I went to see her, she had already heard of the hunting trip on which, it was said everywhere, I was going.

'I am sorry that we cannot amuse Your Majesty here in Strelsau,' she said, a little coldly. 'I would have offered you more entertainment, but I was foolish enough to think – that for a few days – after last night–'

'Yes?'

'That you might be happy without many amusements. I am told you are going to hunt wild pigs. I hope you'll find them interesting.'

I saw a tear fall, and I was angry with myself.

'My dear,' I said. 'Do you dream I should leave you to go hunting?'

'Then – what– ?'

'Well, it is hunting. But Michael is the wild pig.' She turned pale.

'Oh, Rudolf! When will you come back?'

'I – I don't know when I shall come back,' I answered in pain.

'Come soon, Rudolf! Come soon!'

'Yes, by God, I will come again to see you – before I die.'

'What do you mean?'

But I could not tell her the truth then. It was too late.

'Should not a man come back to the loveliest lady in all the world?' said I. 'A thousand Michaels would not keep me from you!'

This comforted her a little.

'You won't let anyone keep you from me?' she asked.

'No, sweetheart.'

But there was one person – not Michael – who, if he lived, would keep me from her, and I was leaving her to risk my own

39

life for his. I could not bear it any longer, and rushed out into the street. I got on my horse and rode off at full speed to my own palace.

The next day I was in the train with Sapt and Fritz and ten gentlemen, specially chosen for the present affair. They had been told something of the story of the attack in the summerhouse, and that Michael was trying to get the throne. They were also informed that a friend of the King's was a prisoner in the Castle of Zenda, and that one of the purposes of the journey was to save him. Young, well-educated, brave and loyal, they asked no more. It was enough that their King needed them, and they were ready to serve him to the death.

We were going to the Castle of Tarlenheim, which belonged to Fritz's uncle. It was a modern building about five miles from Zenda – on the opposite side from that on which Michael's castle lay. It stood on top of a hill with woods all round, in which wild pigs were known to be common. Of course, the real reason we chose it was because it brought us within a short distance of Black Michael.

Michael himself would not be deceived by the story of the hunt. He knew well enough why we had come, and would naturally take steps to prevent us from doing what we wanted.

This was not the only difficulty, for every movement we made was, and had to be, quite public. This was one of the sides of being a king that I found extremely annoying.

Our purpose was to get the King out of the Castle of Zenda alive. Force was useless. Our only chance lay in some trick. We thought, rightly as it appeared, that Michael would not kill the King until he had killed me first. He also probably thought that I was not acting for honour, but for myself. He could not understand a man in my position doing all he could to lose it and put another in his place. My aim in coming to Zenda, in his view, was to get the King killed so that I could have the throne and the

Princess. This gave me courage, because he would keep the King alive as long as he possibly could. And God knows I needed some comfort.

So the journey came to an end, and once more I found myself at Zenda.

Chapter 8 Setting a Trap

Michael knew of my coming, sure enough. I had not been in the Castle of Tarlenheim for an hour when he sent three men to welcome me. He had enough respect for me not to send the men who had tried to murder me, but he sent the other three of his famous Six – the three Ruritanian gentlemen, Lauengram, Krafstein, and Rupert Hentzau. A fine-looking group they made, too, as young Rupert – he could not have been more than twenty-three – took the lead and made me a polite little speech. He said that my dear brother was sorry he could not come himself, but he was ill.

'I am sorry to hear it, sir,' I answered, 'and I trust that no others of his party are sick. I was told that Mr Detchard had been hurt. Is he better?'

Rupert laughed, though his two companions did not.

'He hopes soon to find a medicine for it, sire,' said Rupert.

Then I laughed too. I knew what Detchard's medicine would be.

They then excused themselves, and turned to leave. Rupert, throwing back his black hair, a smile on his good-looking face, walked past Sapt with a scornful look. The old man looked as black as night at him, and lowered his hand to touch his revolver as if by accident.

Instead of dining in the house, I took Fritz out with me to the town to visit the small hotel that I knew of. There was not much

41

danger, since the evening was light and the road along the side of the town was not lonely. I covered my face to prevent the curious from seeing who I was.

'Fritz,' I said as we rode along, 'you will order a private room for two gentlemen of the King. One has a bad toothache. There is a pretty girl at the hotel. You must make sure only she serves us at dinner.'

As we went into the hotel, nothing of my face could be seen except my eyes. Fritz got the room, and went out to see about the girl. A minute later he returned.

'She's coming,' he said.

She came in. I gave her time to put the wine down – I didn't want it dropped. Fritz poured out a glass and gave it to me.

'Is the gentleman in great pain?' the girl asked sympathetically.

'The gentleman is no worse than when he saw you last,' said I, throwing the cover from my face. She gave a little cry; then she said: 'It was the King, then! I told mother so the moment I saw his picture. Oh, sire, forgive me!'

'You did nothing wrong,' said I.

'But the things we said!'

'I forgive them – if you wish to serve the King.'

'Oh, thank you, sire. I must go and tell mother.'

'Stop,' said I, looking serious. 'We are not here tonight for amusement. Go and bring dinner, and not a word to anyone about the King being here.'

She came back in a few minutes, and was naturally very curious.

'How is Johann?' I asked, beginning my dinner.

'Oh, that man, sire – Your Majesty, I mean?'

'"Sire" will do. How is he?'

'We don't see him much now, sire,' she said.

'And why not?'

'I told him he came too often, sire.' She threw back her head.

'I see. But you could bring him back, if you wanted?'

'Perhaps I could, sire. But then he's very busy now at the castle.'

'But there's no shooting or hunting going on just now.'

'No, sire; but he's in charge of the house.'

'Is there no female servant there, then?' I laughed.

'They haven't a woman in the place, sire – not as a servant. They do say – it may be false, sire – that there's a lady there.'

'But Johann would have time to meet you if you asked him?'

'It depends on the time and the place, sire.'

'You don't love him?'

'Not I, sire. But I want to serve Your – the King, sire.'

'All right. Then tell him to meet you two miles outside Zenda tomorrow evening at ten o'clock.'

'You don't mean him any harm, sire?' she asked anxiously.

'Not if he will do as I tell him. Now be off with you, and see that no one knows that the King has been here.'

I spoke severely, but also gave her some money. We finished our dinner, and rode home again.

'You want to catch this man Johann?' said Fritz, when we were outside the town.

'Yes, and I think the trap is going to get him all right.'

As we reached the driveway leading up to the Castle of Tarlenheim, Sapt came rushing to meet us.

'Thank God you're safe,' he said. 'Have you seen anything of them?'

'Of whom?' I asked, getting off my horse.

'My boy,' he said seriously, 'you must not ride around here unless at least six men are with you. You remember a tall young man, one of your guards, called Bernenstein?'

I remembered him all right, about my own height, a fine brave man.

'He is lying upstairs with a bullet through his arm.'

'What!'

'After dinner,' went on Sapt, 'he went out for a walk a mile or so in the wood; he thought he saw three men among the trees and one pointed a gun at him. He was not armed, so he started to run back towards the house. But the man fired at him and hit him. Bernenstein was lucky to get here before he fainted. They were afraid to come nearer the house.' He paused, and added: 'My boy, that bullet was meant for you.'

'Very likely,' I answered. 'Sapt, before I leave Ruritania I should like to do one thing to repay the many kindnesses I have received.'

'What is that?'

'Kill every one of those Six. The country will be a cleaner place.'

◆

Next morning I was sitting in the garden in front of the house, feeling more relaxed than I had been for some time. I was at least doing something; and work, though it cannot cure love, is still a sort of treatment for it. Suddenly through the trees came young Rupert Hentzau, riding as if he was in a public park, careless of any danger there might be from my men. He asked for private speech with me to give me a message from the Duke of Strelsau. I made my friends move away a little.

'Rassendyll,' he said. 'The Duke—'

I sat up. 'Shall I call one of my gentlemen to bring you your horse, my lord?'

'Why keep up the pretence?'

'Because it is not yet finished; and for now I will choose my own name.'

'Oh, all right, sire. But I spoke because of my liking for you. I admire you, you know. You are rather like me.'

'Thank you,' I replied. 'Except that I am honest, loyal to men, and honourable with women, perhaps I am, my lord.'

He looked angrily at me.

'The message?' I asked.

'The Duke offers you more than I would. A safe journey across the border and a hundred thousand pounds.'

'I refuse, of course.'

He smiled at that. 'I told Michael you would,' he said. 'The fact is, between ourselves, Michael doesn't understand a gentleman.'

I laughed. 'And you?' I asked.

'I do,' he answered. 'Well, you prefer death, and you'll have it.'

'I'm sorry you won't live to see it,' said I politely. 'How is your prisoner?'

'The K–?'

'Your prisoner?'

'Oh, I forgot your wishes, sire. He's alive.'

I rose to my feet; he did the same.

'And the pretty princess?' he said, laughingly. 'How's the love affair?'

'Go – while your skin's whole!' I answered angrily, taking a threatening step towards him.

Then came the most daring thing I have seen in my life. My friends were only thirty yards away. Rupert called a servant to bring up his horse. As he was about to get on, he turned to me, putting out his right hand; the left was resting on his belt.

'Shake hands,' he said.

I bowed and did as he knew I would do – put my hands behind me. Quicker than thought, his left hand came out at me, and a small knife flashed in the air. It struck me in the left shoulder; if I had not made a sudden movement, it would have reached my heart. With a cry I took a few steps back and sank into my chair, bleeding deeply. Rupert jumped on to his horse and rode away, followed by cries and revolver shots, the last as useless as the first. Then I fainted.

It was dark when I awoke and found Fritz beside me. I was

weak but cheerful, and more so when Fritz told me the wound was not dangerous and would soon be all right. Then he told me that Johann had fallen into our trap, had been caught and was at that moment in the house.

'What seems strange,' Fritz said, 'is that he is not sorry at being here. He has an idea that when Black Michael has carried out his plan, he will try to get rid of all his helpers, except the Six.'

This showed that our prisoner was not a fool, and I thought his help, if we could get it, would be valuable. I ordered him to be brought up to me at once. Sapt led him in. Johann looked afraid, but after a long talk, during which he seemed to be a weak man rather than a bad one, he agreed to tell us what we wanted to know. Of course we made him generous promises (all of which were kept, so that now he lives in comfort, though I must not tell the place). It also appeared that he had acted as he had more from fear of the Duke and of his own brother Max than for any wish to harm the King. His master, though, believed in him, and Johann knew a good deal of the Duke's plans.

He told us that the King was locked in a small room in the old castle. Next to it was another room, in which there were always three of the Six on guard. If there was an attack on the first room (from which the King's opened), two of the guards would defend it while the other, Rupert or Detchard – for one of these two was always there – would run in and kill the King, who was unarmed and had his hands tied with light steel chains to prevent much movement. So before the outer room was taken by an attacking party, the King would be dead.

'But what about his body?' I asked. For of all things that Michael would not wish anyone to see, the King's body was the most important.

'The Duke has thought of that,' replied Johann. 'Across the window of the King's room, and preventing any light from entering, is the mouth of a large pipe. This is large enough for a

46

man's body to pass down. The pipe curves down to the surface of the moat. When the King is killed, his body will be put down the pipe, weighted so that it will sink at once to the bottom. The guards will then escape, if they can, by sliding down the pipe into the water. They will rise again and swim away, but the King will be at the bottom for ever.'

Johann took a great deal more time to tell the story, and was much less clear, but we got it by asking questions.

'Supposing,' I suggested, 'there is not an armed attack by a few men, but by a whole army that could not be defeated?'

'There would be no defence,' answered Johann. 'The King would be quietly murdered at once, his body put down the pipe, and one of the Six would take his place in the prison, pretending that Michael had put him there. Michael would admit the 'truth' – that the man had angered him, but if he was now sorry, he would set him free.'

Sapt, Fritz and I looked round at one another in shocked surprise at this cruel and clever plan. Whether I went openly with an army, or secretly with a few men, the King would be dead before I could get near him. Michael seemed to have made his success possible and ruin impossible.

'Does the King know?' I asked.

'Yes, sir. When I and my brother were putting up the pipe at the Duke's orders, the King asked Rupert Hentzau what it was, and he said it was his Path to Heaven. It was not suitable for the King to go to Heaven by the common road, he said. Ah, sir, it is not easy to rest peacefully in the Castle of Zenda; all of them would cut a throat as soon as play a game of cards.'

'All right, Johann,' I said. 'If anyone asks you if there is a prisoner in the Castle of Zenda, you may say "Yes". But if they ask you who it is, don't answer. I'll kill you like a dog if the truth about the prisoner becomes known.'

When he was gone I looked at Sapt.

'There seem to be only two ways for the King to be saved,' I said. 'One is by disloyalty in the castle, the other by an act of God!'

Chapter 9   The Path to Heaven

It would have surprised the good people of Ruritania to know of our conversation. According to the official reports, I had been wounded by an accidental blow while hunting. I caused the notices to sound very serious, which resulted in much public excitement. The purpose of this was to make Michael think I was really dangerously wounded and unable to act against him. I learned from Johann that he did believe this. Two other results were that I offended the leading doctors of Strelsau, because I refused to let anyone care for me except a young friend of Fritz's, and I received word from Marshal Strakencz that the Princess Flavia would no longer obey his orders or mine to remain in Strelsau, but was leaving at once for Zenda.

Flavia's arrival, and her joy to find me up and well, instead of on my back fighting with death, is a picture that even now dances before my eyes until they become too full of tears to see it. In truth, to have her with me once more was like a taste of heaven to a criminal who has to die. I was glad to be able to waste two whole days in her company.

It was then that Sapt and I decided that we must risk putting our plan into action, because we heard from Johann that the King was growing thin and ill in his prison. Now a man, whether king or no king, may as well die quickly from a bullet or a knife, as let his life waste away in a prison. That thought made action necessary in the interests of the King. From my own point of view, it grew more necessary still. The Marshal urged me to make arrangements for my marriage. How this affected me may be imagined, since the longer I remained near the princess the more I loved her – and she, it was clear, loved me.

Sapt told me long after that my behaviour at this time was like that of the most powerful ruler; I would allow no criticism, and listen to no advice that did not lead to action. I could see nothing that made life sweet, so I took my life in my hand and carried it as carelessly as a man might carry an old stick.

The next night after our decision, Sapt and I, with Fritz and six men with horses, set out secretly for the Castle of Zenda. Sapt carried a rope, and I took a short heavy stick and a knife. Passing round the town, we went on until we were a quarter of a mile from the old castle. It was a dark stormy night, very suitable for the plan I had in mind.

The six men hid with the horses in the shelter of some trees. Sapt had a whistle to call them if necessary. We had met no one, Michael no doubt thinking I was still really ill in bed. The three of us were now at the edge of the moat, and Sapt tied the rope to a tree. I pulled off my boots, put my stick between my teeth, the knife in my belt, and after a soft 'goodbye', I dropped into the water. I was going to have a look at the Path to Heaven.

Slowly and carefully I swam along by the high dark walls. There were lights in the new part of the castle on the other side, and I heard laughter and merry shouts. No doubt Rupert Hentzau was enjoying himself over his wine.

A dark shape appeared in front of me. It was the pipe. I was near to it when I noticed something else which made my heart stand still. The nose of a boat could be seen on the other side of the pipe. Who was this guarding Michael's invention? Was he awake or asleep? Close by the wall I found there was a narrow shelf of stone under the water. It was part of the base of the castle. I was able to stand on it with my head and shoulders out of the water. Carefully I moved along until I reached the pipe, and then looked round it, where there was a space between it and the wall.

There was a man in the boat. A gun rested beside him. He did not move, and I listened to his breathing. It was heavy and regular. By heaven, he slept! I continued to move along, between the pipe and the wall, until I was within two feet of his face. He was a big man – Max Holf, the brother of Johann. I quietly took the knife from my belt, got as close as I could and prepared to strike.

Of all the things I have done in my life I always hate to think of this. But I said to myself, 'It is war – and the King's life is in danger.' Then I raised the knife and brought it down in his heart. He just had time to open his eyes in fear, but fortunately for me, no time to cry out. He sank back into the boat.

Leaving him where he was, I turned back to the pipe. My time was short, for another guard would probably come soon to take Max's place. I examined the pipe from every side, but could find no crack or opening. But just where the underside went into the wall, covering the window, there was a small ray of light and I heard voices! Detchard was speaking to the King.

'Have you anything to ask, sire, before I leave you for the night?'

The King's voice followed. It was his, though it was faint, nothing like the merry one I had heard in the forest and at the lodge.

'Ask my brother,' said the King, 'to kill me. I am dying here day by day.'

'The Duke does not desire your death, sire – yet,' replied Detchard scornfully. 'When he does, this is your Path to Heaven!'

The light disappeared, and I heard the sound of the door being locked. It was too dangerous to try to speak to the King. He might give a shout of surprise. So I climbed into the boat to remove Max's body. The storm was blowing more loudly now, so I was able to row fast.

I came to the tree, and as I did so, a whistle sounded over the moat behind me.

'Hullo, Max!' someone shouted.

'Quick, Sapt,' I said. I tied the rope round the body, and when I had climbed up myself we pulled up Max.

'Whistle for our men,' I said. 'No talk now.'

Sapt did so, but just then three men on horseback came along the road from the castle. We saw them but, being on foot, we could not be seen. We heard our own men coming up from the other direction with a shout.

'It's as dark as the devil,' said someone, and I recognized Rupert's voice. The next moment shots rang out. Our men had met them and we ran forward to join in the fight. Shouts and cries of pain showed that someone at least was hit. Suddenly a horse came towards me, and I ran to its head. It was Rupert Hentzau.

'At last!' I cried.

We seemed to have him. He had only his sword in his hand. My men were close behind him. Sapt and Fritz were not far away, but I had run faster than they.

'At last!' I cried again.

'It's the play-actor!' cried he, using his sword against my stick, which he cut into two. I thought he would have me then, so jumped out of reach of his blows. The devil was in Rupert; for urging his horse forward, he went straight for the moat and jumped in, the shots of our party falling all round him. With one ray of moonlight we could have shot him, but it was as black as ink, and in the darkness he swam with his horse to the corner of the castle wall and escaped.

'What's happened?' I asked.

'Lauengram and Krafstein both killed, sire,' said one of my men.

'And Max,' said I. 'That's three of them.'

As it was impossible to hide what had taken place, we threw the bodies into the moat. Then we found that three of my gentlemen had also been killed. We carried their bodies home with us. We were heavy at heart for the death of our friends, troubled about the King, and annoyed at the second success young Rupert had gained over us.

As for me, I was also ashamed that I had killed no man in open fight, nor was I pleased to hear Rupert call me a play-actor.

◆

It was impossible to keep secret the deaths of so many gentlemen, so I gave out a strict order that no private fighting would be allowed in future. I also sent a note to Michael saying how sorry I was, and he sent me one; our one point of union was that neither of us could tell the truth about the other. Unfortunately for me, secrecy meant delay. The King might die in prison, or even be carried off somewhere else.

One of the strange results of the necessity of being friendly to Michael in public was that the town of Zenda became, in the daytime, a place where both sides could meet safely. By night it was doubtless a different manner. Riding down one day with Flavia and Sapt, we had a meeting which in one way was rather amusing, but in another rather difficult for me. An important-looking person in a carriage got out and came towards me. It was the Chief of the Strelsau Police.

'Your Majesty's orders about fighting are being carefully attended to,' he said.

'Is that what brings you to Zenda?' I asked, determined that he would have to go back to Strelsau at once. His presence might prove annoying.

'Why no, sire. I am here at the request of the British ambassador.'

'Whatever does he want?' I asked carelessly, but secretly anxious.

'A young countryman of his, sire, a man of some rank, is

missing. His friends have not heard from him for two months, and there is reason to believe that he was last seen in Zenda.'

Flavia was not paying attention. I dared not look at Sapt.

'What reason?'

'A friend of his in Paris has told us that it is possible he came here, and the railway officials here remember his name on his luggage.'

'What was his name?'

'Rassendyll, sire.' With a quick look at Flavia he lowered his voice. 'It is thought he followed a lady here. Has Your Majesty heard of Madame de Mauban?'

'Why, yes,' said I, my eye travelling to the castle.

'She arrived in Ruritania about the same time as this Rassendyll.'

'You are suggesting?'

'Supposing he were in love with the lady?' he whispered. 'Nothing has been heard of him for two months.' This time it was his eye that travelled towards the castle.

'Yes, the lady is there,' I said quietly. 'But I don't suppose this gentleman – Rassendyll, did you say his name was? – is there too.'

'The Duke does not like competition, sire.'

'You are suggesting something very serious,' I said. 'You had better go straight back to Strelsau.'

'To Strelsau? But it is here, sire, that–'

'Go back to Strelsau,' I repeated. 'Tell the ambassador that you have information, and will tell him in a week's time of the result of your inquiries.'

'The ambassador is pressing for action, sire.'

'You must quiet him. At the same time I will look into the matter here myself.'

He promised to obey me, and to leave that night. At all costs inquiries after me must be stopped for a week or two, and this clever official had come surprisingly near the truth.

Chapter 10   A Dangerous Plan

Just as we were turning to ride back to Tarlenheim, we saw a procession coming from the Castle of Zenda. First came two servants on horseback, then a funeral carriage and, behind it, a man in plain black clothes.

'It's Rupert,' whispered Sapt.

Rupert it was and, seeing us, he left his party and rode towards us, bowing respectfully.

'Who is the dead man, my lord?' I asked.

'My friend Lauengram,' he replied sadly, but a quick smile shot for a moment across his face as he saw Sapt's hand in his pocket. He guessed – and rightly – that Sapt held a revolver.

'Was the poor man killed in the fight?' asked Flavia.

'Sir,' I said, 'no one is sorrier about the affair than I.'

'Your Majesty's words are kind,' he replied. 'I am sorry for my friend. But, sire, others may soon lie as he lies now.'

'True,' said I. 'We should all remember it.'

'Even kings, sire,' added Rupert daringly. He moved off. With a sudden thought I rode after him. He turned quickly, fearing that, even in the presence of the dead, and in front of a lady's eyes, I would harm him.

'You fought as a brave man the other night,' I said. 'Come, you are young, sir. If you will give up your prisoner alive to me, you shall come to no hurt, I swear to you.'

He looked at me with a scornful smile.

'Look here,' he said, 'you refused an offer from Black Michael. Hear one from me.' He lowered his voice. 'Attack the castle openly. Let Sapt and Tarlenheim lead.'

'Go on,' said I.

'Arrange the time with me.'

'I have such confidence in you, my lord!'

'Listen to me! I'm talking business now. Sapt and Fritz will fall;

54

Black Michael will fall–'

'What!'

'Black Michael will fall, like the dog he is. The prisoner, as you call him, will go down the Path to Heaven – ah, you know that! – and only two men will be left, I, Rupert of Hentzau, and you, the King of Ruritania.'

He paused and then, in a voice shaking with eagerness, went on, 'Is not that a plan to try? For you a throne and a princess! For me, a high position and Your Majesty's thanks.'

'Surely,' I cried, 'while you're still alive, the devil has no master.'

'Well, think it over,' he said. 'It would take more than any feeling of honour to keep me from that girl–'

'Get out of my reach!' I said; though in a moment I began to laugh at the daring of the man. But Rupert did not move. He just smiled nastily.

'Would you turn against your master?' I asked.

He swore at Michael, and said, 'He gets in my way, you know. He's a jealous fool! I nearly stuck a knife in him last night.'

I was learning something now, so I asked carelessly, 'A lady?'

'Yes, and a beautiful one; but you've seen her.'

'Ah! Was it at a tea party when some of your friends got on the wrong side of the table?'

'That fool Detchard. If only I had been there!'

'And the Duke is interested?'

'Well,' said Rupert, laughing, 'I'm the one who is interested. Michael doesn't like it. She prefers him, the foolish creature. Well, think over my proposal.'

He went off to rejoin his procession, and I rode home with Flavia, thinking about men's evil ways. Of all the men I had ever met, Rupert was certainly the most evil!

As we reached the Castle of Tarlenheim, a boy handed me a note. I tore it open and read:

I warned you once. In the name of God, and if you are a man, save me from this house of murderers!

A. DE M.

I handed it to Sapt, but all he said was: 'Whose fault brought her there?'

Although I felt sorry for her, I seemed as powerless to help her as I had been to help the King. Matters soon became worse, as, in addition to the danger of the police inquiries about my disappearance, there was a more urgent problem. People at Strelsau were already talking about my absence from the city, and Marshal Strakencz came with the Chancellor to ask me to fix a day for my engagement, which in Ruritania was as final as the marriage ceremony itself.

Flavia was sitting by me, and so I was forced to choose a day two weeks ahead. This caused great happiness all through the kingdom, so that only two men in the country were annoyed – I mean Black Michael and myself – and only one did not know of it – the King.

We heard from Johann how the news was received at the Castle of Zenda, but we heard something more important. The King was very sick; in fact, he was too weak to move. They had sent for a doctor, who was terribly frightened at what he saw, but the Duke kept him a prisoner in the same room as the King. Antoinette de Mauban had also been helping to nurse the sick man, since it was quite clear that his life was in danger. And here was I, strong, healthy – and free.

'And how do they guard the King now?' I asked Johann.

'Detchard and Bersonin watch by night, Rupert Hentzau and de Gautet by day, sir, except that the Duke will never allow Rupert Hentzau to be there when Madame de Mauban is with the King, sir.'

Johann begged us to keep him at Tarlenheim, but we gave him

more money and persuaded him to return to tell Antoinette that we were doing all we could, and if possible she should speak some words of comfort to the King, for nothing is worse for the sick than hopelessness.

We got an exact statement from Johann about where the different people in the castle slept. The two of the Six (now only Four) who were not guarding the King lay in a room just above. It was reached by some steps from just inside the main door. Michael himself had a room in the new castle on the first floor, and Madame de Mauban had one too. The Duke locked her door after she had gone in – I understood why after my conversation with Rupert. The drawbridge was pulled back at night, and only Michael had the key.

'And where do you sleep?' I asked Johann.

'In the entrance hall of the new castle, sir, with the other servants.'

'Listen,' I said. 'I have promised you twenty thousand silver pieces. You shall have fifty thousand if you will do what I ask of you tomorrow night. At two o'clock in the morning exactly, you must open the front door. Say you want some fresh air, or anything you like. Do not fail by a moment.'

'Will you be there, sir?'

'Ask no questions. That is all I want you to do.'

'May I escape when I open the door?'

'Yes, as quickly as your legs will carry you. One thing more – carry this note to Madame de Mauban, and tell her that all our lives depend on her doing exactly what it says.'

The man was shaking, but I had to trust to what he had of courage and to what he had of honesty. I dared not wait, and as I had failed at the Path to Heaven, I must try the other side.

I then called Sapt and Fritz and explained my plan. Sapt shook his head.

'Why can't you wait?' he asked.

57

'The King may die.'

'Michael will have to act before that happens; is he going to leave you on the throne?'

'It's not only that. Supposing the King does live – for two weeks more?'

Sapt bit his moustache. Fritz put his hand on my shoulder.

'You are right, Rudolf,' he said. 'Let us go and make the attempt.'

'Fritz and I will go,' said Sapt. 'Then if we fail, and Michael kills the King – us, too – you will still be alive to rule.'

'No,' I said. 'I have been a deceiver for another. I will not be one for my own profit. If the King is not alive on the engagement day, I will tell the world the truth, whatever happens.'

'You shall go too, my boy,' said Sapt.

This was my plan:

A strong party under Sapt's command would move quietly up to the door of the new castle. If they met anyone on the way, they must kill them, with swords if possible to avoid noise. When Johann opened the door, they would rush in and seize the servants. At the same moment – and the whole plan depended on this – a woman's cry would ring out loud and clear from Antoinette de Mauban's room. Again and again she would cry, 'Help! Help! Michael, help! It's Rupert Hentzau!' Then Michael, we hoped, would rush out of his room near by, and fall into the hands of Sapt and his men. Still the cries would go on. My men, getting the key from Michael, would send the drawbridge across. It would be strange if Rupert, hearing his name being used falsely, did not run down from his room and cross the bridge to see what the matter was. De Gautet might or might not come with him; we had to leave that to chance.

And when Rupert was on the bridge? That was my part. I was going to swim in the moat again and hide by the bridge. Rupert – and de Gautet, if he came too – would be killed by me in the

58

dark. There would be only two men left, and we would have the keys. We must rush into the room where Detchard and Bersonin were, and trust, in the general confusion, that they would defend themselves instead of obeying their orders to kill the King first. There was a further chance that, hearing what he imagined to be a quarrel between Michael and Rupert, Detchard would leave only Bersonin to guard the King, and cross the drawbridge himself to help Michael.

That was the plan – and only a lack of any other ideas drove us to it. To hide our preparations a little, I had the whole of the Castle of Tarlenheim brightly lit, as if we were dancing and enjoying ourselves.

I ordered Marshal Strakencz, if we did not return by morning, to march openly to the Castle of Zenda, demand to see the King, and if he did not see him, to take Flavia with him to Strelsau at once and announce that she was Queen, telling the country that Black Michael had killed the King.

To tell the truth, that was what I thought most likely to happen, since I did not think that Michael, the King or I had more than another day to live.

It was late when we had finished making our arrangements, so I went to say good night to Flavia. I took off a ring I had – a family ring – and gave it to her.

'Wear that ring even though you will wear another when you are Queen,' I said.

'Whatever else I wear, I will wear this until I die,' said she, as she kissed the ring. And there were tears in her eyes and in mine.

Chapter 11   Rupert and Michael

The night was fine and clear. I had wished for bad weather like I had on my first trip, but it was not to be. I thought, though, that by keeping close under the wall of the old castle I should not be seen from the windows of the new building across the moat. They might search the moat, but it was unlikely. Johann had told me that the big pipe had been strengthened, and could not be moved. Even if Johann was not loyal to us, he did not know my plan and would expect to see me with my friends at the front door when he opened it at two o'clock.

At midnight Sapt's party left, going secretly through the woods to the Castle of Zenda. If all went well, they would be at the front door at a quarter to two. If the door was not opened, Fritz would go round the other side of the castle and meet me, if I was still alive. If I failed to meet him, they were to return to Tarlenheim, collect as much force as possible, and attack the castle. For if I was not there to meet Fritz, I would be dead. And that would mean that the King, too, would be killed a few seconds after me.

I myself set out alone. I was warmly dressed, for there was no need to become so cold in the water of the moat that I might be unable to do my part properly. I carried a light rope and a small silk ladder to help me to get out of the moat. I went a shorter way than the others; at about half past twelve I got off my horse and tied it to a tree out of sight, and then went down to the moat.

I tied the rope to a tree trunk, and let myself into the water. As I began to swim slowly along, I heard the castle clock strike a quarter to one. After a few minutes I came to the Path to Heaven, in the shadow of which I waited. Ten yards away I could see the drawbridge; it was still in its place. I could see, on the other side of the moat, the windows of the Duke's and Madame de Mauban's rooms, if Johann had explained correctly.

Suddenly the Duke's window became bright. It was open, and Antoinette herself looked out. I wanted to cry, 'Remember!' but I dared not. A moment later a man came up and stood beside her; she jumped away from him, and then I heard a low laugh. It was

Rupert! A moment afterwards I saw him. He was whispering to Antoinette.

'Gently, gently!' I said quietly. 'You're too soon, my boy!'

Rupert came and looked out. 'Hang Black Michael!' I heard him say. 'Isn't the Princess enough for him? Is he to have everything? What the devil do you see in Black Michael?'

'If I told him what you say—' she began.

'Well, tell him,' said Rupert carelessly. Then he suddenly moved forward and kissed her. He laughed, and cried, 'There's something to tell him!'

The unhappy woman raised her hands above her head, in prayer or in hopelessness.

'Do you know what he's promised me, if I cut the play-actor's throat?' Rupert went on. 'He'll take the Princess, and I — but I don't want to wait, that's all.'

I heard the noise of a door opening, and then Black Michael's voice: 'What are you doing here, sir?'

He came to the window, and took Rupert by the arm.

'The moat can hold more than the King,' said Black Michael angrily.

'Do you threaten me, my lord?' asked Rupert daringly.

'A threat is more warning than most men get from me,' answered Michael.

'But Rudolf Rassendyll has been much threatened, and still lives.'

'Am I at fault because my servants make stupid mistakes?'

'*You* have not yet run any risk of making mistakes,' said Rupert scornfully.

The message was as plain as it could possibly be. Black Michael had self-control, though. His voice was quite calm as he answered: 'Enough, enough! We mustn't quarrel, Rupert. Are Detchard and Bersonin at their posts?'

'They are, sir.'

61

'I need you no more.'

'Oh, I'm not tired,' said Rupert.

'Sir, please leave us. In ten minutes the drawbridge will be pulled back and I suppose you don't want to swim to your bed.'

Rupert's figure disappeared. I heard the door open and shut. Michael and Antoinette were no longer to be seen. Then I heard Rupert's voice from the end of the bridge.

'De Gautet, unless you want a bath before your bed, come along!'

A moment later the two men crossed the drawbridge, and as soon as they were over, it was pulled back. The clock struck a quarter past one.

I think some ten minutes had passed when I heard a slight noise near me, beyond the pipe. I was surprised to see that it was Rupert in the doorway of the old castle. He came towards me, then climbed down some steps cut in the wall that I had not noticed before. He had a sword between his teeth. If it had been a matter of my life only, I would have swum to meet him, for I would have loved to fight it out with him then and there! But I kept myself back, since it was the King's life that I was there to save.

He swam quietly and easily across the moat, and climbed up by the gate to the new castle. I heard him unlock the door, and then he disappeared inside. Clearly there were other plans as well as mine being acted on in the castle that night.

It immediately came to my mind that whatever evil act Rupert was busy with, the fact that he was out of the old castle was a great advantage to me. It left only three men for me to deal with. Ah! If I only had the keys!

There was still a light in Antoinette's window, but Michael's was dark. He was no doubt fast asleep in bed by now. Then, from across the moat, I heard the sound of a door being unlocked – slowly and quietly. I was just asking myself what on earth it was when I got the answer. Before my friends could be near the main door of the new castle, before Johann would have thought to go near to open it, there was a sudden crash from Antoinette's room. It sounded as though someone had thrown down a lamp; at the same moment the room went dark. Then a cry rang out loud through the night: 'Help! Help! Michael, help!'

Angry that I could do nothing, I climbed up the stone steps and stood in the gateway of the old castle. At least, no one could come in or out without meeting me.

There was another cry from Antoinette. Then Michael's door was thrown open, and I heard the Duke's voice shouting: 'Open the door! In God's name, what's the matter?' There was the sound of a door handle being twisted fiercely. He was answered in the very words I had written in my letter: 'Help, Michael! It's Rupert Hentzau!'

I heard the door broken open, then the ringing sound of crossed swords. At the same time, a window above my head opened, and De Gautet's voice cried out, 'What's the matter?' It all happened so quickly that it is impossible to tell it clearly. Everything seemed to happen at the same time. Antoinette's window was thrown open, and I heard the cry of a wounded man. Then Rupert appeared in sight, his back to the window, and he was fighting hard.

'Ah, Johann, there's one for you! Come on, Michael!'

Johann was there, then, come to save the Duke! How would he open the front door?

'Help!' cried the Duke's voice, weak and faint.

There were footsteps on the stairs behind me, but before anyone came out, I saw Rupert with five or six men round him. Suddenly he jumped onto the window, and remained there for a second, laughing like a man, drunk with blood. Then he threw himself straight into the moat.

At the same moment, de Gautet's face appeared in the door

beside me. I struck at him with all my strength, and he fell dead in the doorway. Quickly I searched him for the keys. At last I had them. There were only three. I tried one in the door leading to the King's room. It was the right one! I unlocked the door as quietly as I could, passed through, and relocked it behind me. There were some steps in front of me as I saw from an oil-lamp on the wall. I took down the lamp and listened.

'Whatever is it?' I heard a voice say from behind a door that faced me at the bottom of the stairs. Another answered: 'Shall we kill him?'

There was a pause – terrible enough for me – then Detchard said: 'Wait a bit. There'll be trouble if we do it too soon.'

A moment later I heard the door being unlocked, and I put out the lamp, replacing it on the wall.

'It's dark,' Bersonin said. 'The lamp's out. Give me that one.'

The moment for action had arrived.

I rushed down the steps and threw myself at the door, which swung open. Bersonin stood there, sword in hand. Detchard was sitting on a chair. In his surprise at seeing me, Bersonin fell back a step or two. Detchard jumped to his sword. I rushed at the Belgian, and drove him against the wall. He was a brave man, but no swordsman, and in a moment he lay on the floor before me. I turned. Detchard was not there. Following orders, he had not risked a fight with me, but had run straight into the inner room and locked the door behind him. Even now he was at his work inside.

And surely he would have killed the King, and perhaps me too, if it had not been for one loyal man who gave his life for the King. When I broke the door in, the sight I saw was this. The King stood in the corner of the room. Weak from his sickness, he could do nothing but move his tied hands uselessly up and down; he was even laughing like a man going crazy. Detchard and the doctor were in the middle of the room, and the doctor had thrown himself on the murderer. He held Detchard's arms to his sides for a moment. Then Detchard forced himself free and, as I entered, he drove his sword through the unfortunate man.

Then he turned on me, crying: 'At last!'

We were sword to sword. By a happy chance neither he nor Bersonin had been wearing their revolvers. I found them afterwards on a shelf near the door; my sudden rush had prevented them from reaching them. Yes, we were man to man; and we began to fight silently and hard. He was a better swordsman than I, and slowly he forced me back against the wall. I saw a smile on his face, and he wounded me in the left arm.

I deserve no praise for winning the fight, since he was the best swordsman I have ever met and he would certainly have killed me and then done his murderer's work if we had been alone. But just then, the King, weak as he was, began jumping up and down, crying: 'It's Brother Rudolf! I'll help you, Brother Rudolf!' He picked up a chair and came towards us.

'Come on!' I cried. 'Come on! Drive it against his legs.'

The King laughed and came forward, holding the chair in front of him.

With an angry cry, Detchard jumped back, and before I knew what he was doing, had turned his sword against the King. He made one fierce cut, and the King, with a cry, dropped to the floor. Then Detchard was at me again, but his own hand had prepared his destruction; as he turned he stepped in the blood flowing from the dead doctor.

He slipped and fell. Before he could stand again I was on him, and I drove my point through his neck. He fell heavily across the body of the loyal doctor.

Was the King dead? It was my first thought. I rushed to where he lay, and tried to listen to his heart, but just then I heard a sound that brought me to my feet in a second. It was the drawbridge being pulled across. I would be caught like a rat in a trap, and the

King with me, if he was still alive. He must take his chance now.

As I passed into the other room, I saw the revolvers, and took one. At the door of the outer room I paused to listen. Who was pushing the drawbridge across? My friends? I would have given the world to hear Sapt's voice, as I stood there trying to get my breath and tying up my wound with a piece torn from my shirt.

Thinking that I could defend the narrow door at the top of the steps better than this one, I dragged myself up there and paused again.

Then came a strange sound – strange for the time and place. It was an easy, scornful laugh – the laugh of young Rupert Hentzau! I could hardly believe that any man could laugh, but it told me that my men had not come, for they would have shot Rupert before this. The clock struck half past two! My God! The door had not been opened! They had gone to the place where I had to meet Fritz and not found me! By now I supposed they were back at Tarlenheim with the news of the King's death – and mine.

Chapter 12   Face to Face in the Forest

For a moment or two I sank discouraged against the door. Then I jumped up again, as Rupert cried: 'Well, the bridge is there! Come over it! Let's see Black Michael. Keep back, you dogs! Michael, come and fight for her!'

If there was to be a fight, I might still do something, so I turned the key in the main door and looked out.

It was a strange scene. At the far end of the bridge was a group of the Duke's servants, some holding lights, others armed with old-fashioned steel weapons. They were pale and frightened; all in fact, afraid at the sight of Rupert standing in the middle of the bridge, his sword in his hand. At the back I saw Johann holding a cloth to a wound in his face. They dared not move forward.

By a lucky chance I was master. The frightened servants would not oppose me any more than they dared attack Rupert. I had only to raise my revolver to shoot him dead, since he had no idea that I was there. But I did nothing – why, I hardly know to this day. I had killed one man from behind that night, and another by luck rather than skill – perhaps it was that. Also, evil as the man was, I did not like being one of a crowd against him – perhaps it was that. But stronger than either of these feelings was one of curiosity. I just wanted to see what would happen.

'Michael, you dog! If you can stand, come on!' cried Rupert. The answer to this came in the wild cry of a woman: 'He's dead! My God, he's dead!'

'Dead!' shouted Rupert. 'I struck better than I knew.' And he laughed victoriously. Then he went on: 'Down with your weapons there! I'm your master now. Down with them, I say!'

I believe they would have obeyed, but as he spoke distant shouts and knockings came from the other side of the new castle. My heart jumped with joy. It must be my men, come by a fortunate disobedience to find me. The noise continued, but no one seemed to pay attention, for just then Antoinette herself pushed through the servants and came on to the bridge. She was in a loose white nightdress, her dark hair streamed over her shoulders, her face was deathly pale and her eyes shone wildly. In her shaking hands she held a revolver, which she raised and fired at Rupert. The shot missed him and struck the wooden door above my head.

'Well, madam,' laughed Rupert, 'if your eyes had been no more dangerous than your shooting, I should not be in this position – nor Black Michael dead – tonight!'

She tried to calm herself, and aimed at him steadily. He would be crazy to risk it. Thinking he would run towards me, I aimed my own revolver at him.

But crying, 'I cannot kill where I've kissed,' Rupert jumped over the bridge into the moat. At the same moment I heard a rush of feet, and a voice I knew – it was Sapt's – shout: 'God! It's the Duke – dead!'

Then I knew that the King needed me no more and, throwing away my revolver, I jumped on to the bridge. There was a cry of surprise from the group of servants – 'The King!' – and then I, like Rupert, jumped into the moat.

I saw him fifteen yards ahead. He swam easily and well. I was tired out and wounded. I could not go so fast. As we reached the corner of the castle wall, I called out to him: 'Stop, Rupert, stop!' I saw him look over his shoulder, but he didn't stop, nor did he recognize me in the dark. There was no way to climb out of the moat except by the rope that I had tied to the tree. Rupert might find it, or he might not.

I soon knew. I heard him say: 'How the devil did this get here?' Then he took hold of the rope and pulled himself out. At the same moment I arrived, and he saw me.

'Hullo! Who's here?' he cried in surprise. 'Why, it's the play-actor! How did you arrive here, man?'

I took hold of the rope, but I paused. He stood on the bank, sword in hand, and he could cut my head open as I came up.

'Never mind,' said I, 'but as I am here, I think I'll stay.'

He smiled down at me. 'These women –' he began; when suddenly the great bell of the castle started to ring, and a loud shout reached us. Rupert waved his hand to me.

'I would like a fight with you, but it's a little too dangerous,' said he, and off he went.

In a second I was climbing the rope. I was up. I saw him thirty yards away, running like a deer towards the shelter of the forest. For once Rupert preferred wisdom to daring. I rushed after him, calling him to stand and fight. He would not. Unwounded and strong, he got farther and farther from me at every step; but forgetting everything in the world except him and my thirst for his blood, I continued, and soon the deep shades of the forest of Zenda swallowed us both.

It was three o'clock now, and day was breaking. I was on a long straight grass .path, and a hundred yards in front ran young Rupert. He looked over his shoulder and waved scornfully, since he saw that I could not catch him. A moment later he disappeared from my sight, and I thought it was all over.

I was just sinking to the ground from tiredness when I heard a cry ring through the forest – a woman's cry. With the last of my strength, I ran on, and saw him again. He was in the act of lifting a girl down from her horse. It was her cry I had heard. She was a farmer's daughter, I thought, on the way to Zenda market. He treated her gently, gave her a kiss and some money, but did not leave immediately. He waited for me.

'What did you do in the castle?' he asked as I came near.

'I killed three of your friends,' said I.

'What! You got to the King's room?'

'Yes, and I pray that he still lives. I killed Detchard.'

'You fool!' he said pleasantly.

'One thing more I did, I did not kill you when I could have. I was behind you on the bridge with a revolver in my hand.'

'Then I was between two fires?'

'Get off your horse,' I said, 'and fight like a man.'

'What? In front of a lady?' he laughed.

Then, in my anger, hardly knowing what I did, I rushed at him. He froze for a moment, and I struck at him with my sword. I reached his face, and he was surprised by my fierceness. But before he could ride at me and finish me off, there was a shout from behind me, and I saw a man on a horse. It was Fritz von Tarlenheim, and he was riding hard. Rupert knew that the game was over. He cried: 'Goodbye, Rassendyll!'

And with his face streaming blood, he bowed to me and rode

off at full speed. Fritz fired a shot at him, and struck his sword, which fell to the ground. Away he rode, and I watched him go; he was laughing, and once he turned to wave his hand. So he disappeared – careless but careful, graceful but without honour, good-looking but evil, evil but unbeaten.

I threw my sword on the ground and cried to Fritz to go after him. But Fritz stopped his horse, jumped down and ran to me. And it was time, because the wound Detchard had given me was bleeding again.

'Then give me the horse,' I cried and, trying to get to my feet, I fell full length on the ground. Fritz knelt beside me.

'Fritz!' I said.

'Yes, friend,' he answered, as gently as a woman.

'Is the King alive?'

He wiped my lips. 'Thanks to the bravest gentleman that lives,' said he softly, 'the King is alive.'

The little farm girl stood by us, crying from fear and confusion, and I tried to cheer but could not. Tired and cold, I just laid my head back in Fritz's arm and fell asleep.

◆

I learned afterwards the full story of what happened on that night in the Castle of Zenda. Antoinette told how there had been quarrels between Rupert and Michael about her before, and this last one was only one of many. Rupert, coming to her room when he knew that Michael had gone, made her cry out for help before the planned time. At first this seemed to have ruined our hopes, but as it happened it helped them. Rupert and Michael had fought, but Rupert had jumped from the window without knowing that he had killed his master. As for Sapt and Fritz, they had arrived at the castle door as arranged, and had waited until half past two. Then, according to my orders, Sapt had sent Fritz to search the banks of the moat. I was not there. Hurrying back,

Fritz told Sapt, who wanted to ride back at full speed to Tarlenheim, as I had said. Fritz, though, would not hear of it, orders or no orders. So they sent a party back to Tarlenheim to fetch the Marshal, while the rest attacked the door of the new castle. They broke in just as Antoinette was firing at Rupert. The first door they came to was that of Michael's room, and there was the Duke lying dead.

Sapt and Fritz then crossed the bridge, not knowing what had happened to me or the King, since Antoinette could tell them nothing except that she had seen me on the bridge. At last they reached the outer room and found the Belgian, Bersonin, lying dead, and Sapt said: 'Thank God, he has been here.' When they found Detchard and the doctor, and the King also seemingly dead, at first they thought it was all over. But Sapt, who knew more of wounds and the signs of death than I, recognized that the King was not badly hurt and would soon be well again.

Then Fritz was sent to look for me – Sapt dared send no one else, and how he found me you have heard. Fritz was guided by the shout which I made, calling on Rupert to stop. And I think a man has never been more glad to find his own brother alive than was Fritz to find me.

It now only remained to make sure that the secret was kept. Antoinette and Johann swore to say nothing. Fritz, it was said, had ridden off to find the King's friend, held by the Duke in the Castle of Zenda. The King, having saved his friend, had been wounded almost to death, and lay at Zenda. The Princess was ordered to remain at Tarlenheim until the King could come to her. So ran Sapt's story, and it was believed everywhere. The only thing to upset it was a force that often defeats the cleverest of plans – I mean the pleasure of a woman.

For whatever the King might command (or Sapt for him), the Princess Flavia refused to remain at Tarlenheim while her lover was wounded at Zenda. So she drove in her carriage behind

Marshal Strakencz, who tried without success to make her stay at home. In this way she came to the edge of the forest, where I still lay. Just as I awoke from my faint, I saw her and, understanding what I ought to do, I tried to hide behind a bush. We had forgotten the farm girl, though. She ran to the Princess, crying: 'Madam, the King is here – in the bushes!'

'Nonsense, child,' said old Marshal Strakencz, 'The King lies wounded at the castle over there.'

'Yes, sir, I know he's wounded,' said the girl, 'but he's here with Count Fritz von Tarlenheim, not at the castle.'

The girl told what she had seen, and Flavia, smiling at her, climbed down from her carriage to see who the gentleman was that looked like the King. At that moment Sapt appeared, riding from the castle, and tried to persuade the Princess to continue her journey.

'Every fine gentleman is a king to girls like this,' he said.

'Why, he's as like the King as one bean to another!' cried the girl in surprise.

The Marshal's face asked unspoken questions. Flavia, too, looked round at them. Doubt spread quickly.

'I'll see this man,' said Flavia.

'Then come alone,' whispered Sapt.

She was obedient to the strangeness of his voice, and told the Marshal and the others to wait. She and Sapt came forward on foot towards where we lay. Sapt waved the farm girl away. I could not look at her, and buried my face in my hands. Fritz knelt by me, his hand on my shoulder.

'It is he! Are you hurt?' was Flavia's cry, half of joy, half of fear.

She sat on the ground by me, and gently pulled my hands away.

'It is the King!' she said. 'Why did you try to deceive me just now, Colonel?'

No one answered her, and I kept my eyes on the ground. Then

she put her arm on mine. 'Rudolf—' she began.

'It is not the King,' said Sapt. His voice was almost gentle.

Fritz's pale face told her that it was true.

'But it is Rudolf, my love,' she cried.

'It is your love, madam, but not the King. The King lies there in the Castle of Zenda.'

'Look at me, Rudolf,' she cried. 'Why do you let them say such things?'

Then I spoke, looking into her eyes.

'God forgive me, madam,' I said. 'I am not the King.'

Her face went even whiter. She looked at Sapt, at Fritz, then again at me. Then she fell forward and fainted. I laid her softly on the ground, deeply unhappy that Rupert's sword had left me alive to bear this.

Chapter 13   If Love Were All!

It was night, and I was in the little room which had been the King's prison. Fritz had brought me here secretly. Johann had just come in with some supper and he told me what was going on in the castle. When I was tired of Johann's talk, I sent him away, and Fritz came to visit me. He said the King wanted to see me, so we crossed the drawbridge and entered the room that had been Black Michael's.

The King was lying there in bed. The doctor (Fritz's friend from Tarlenheim) said the visit must be a short one. The King held out his hand and shook mine. Fritz and the doctor went to the window. I took the King's ring from my finger and placed it on his.

'I have tried not to dishonour it, sire,' said I.

'I can't talk much,' he said in a weak voice. 'I wanted to keep you here with me, but Sapt and the Marshal say it is impossible, and that the secret must be kept.'

'They are right, sire. Let me go. My work here is done.'

'Yes, it is done, as no man but you could have done it. When they see me again, I shall have my beard on; I shall be changed with sickness. But I shall try to let them find me changed in nothing but appearance. You have shown me how to be a king.'

His eyelids closed. He was tired. I kissed his hand, and Fritz came to lead me away. I have never seen the King since.

Outside, Fritz did not turn the way we had come, but went another way.

'Where are we going?' I asked.

'She has sent for you. When it is over, come back to the bridge. I'll wait there.'

'What does she want?' I asked breathlessly. He shook his head. 'Does she know everything?'

'Yes, everything.'

He opened a door, gently pushed me in, and left me. It was a room filled with beautiful furniture, and in the middle of it stood the Princess. I walked up to her and fell on one knee and kissed her hand. Then, before I knew what I was saying, the word came out: 'Flavia!'

She shook a little as I rose to my feet and faced her.

'Don't stand, don't stand!' she cried. 'You mustn't! You're hurt. Sit down here – on this chair.'

She gently made me sit, and put her hand on my forehead.

'How hot your head is!' she said.

I had come to beg for her forgiveness, but somehow love gives to even a dull man the knowledge of his lover's heart. So all I said was: 'I love you with all my heart and soul!'

For what troubled and shamed her? Not her love for me, but the fear that I had pretended to love her as I had pretended to be the King.

'I love you,' I repeated. 'There will never be another woman in the world for me. But God forgive me the wrong I've done!'

'They made you do it,' she said quickly. 'It might have made no difference if I'd known. It was always you that I loved, never the King.'

'I tried to tell you – you remember when Sapt interrupted us on the night of the dance at Strelsau?'

'I know,' she answered softly. 'They have told me all.'

'I am going away tonight,' I said.

'No, no, no! Not tonight!'

'I must, before more people have seen me. And how could I stay–'

'If I could come with you!' she whispered.

'Don't,' I cried, almost roughly, and moved away from her.

'You are right, Rudolf, dear,' she said. 'If love were all, I would follow you to the world's end. But is love the only thing? If it were, you would have left the King to die in his prison.'

'I nearly did it, Flavia,' I whispered.

'But honour did not let you. Women too must behave honourably, Rudolf. My honour lies in being loyal to my country. I shall always wear your ring.'

'And I yours,' I answered. Then I said goodbye and left her. I heard her saying my name over and over again . . .

Rapidly I walked down to the bridge. Sapt and Fritz were both there. I rode off with them through the forest. We came to a little station on the other side of the border, and had to wait for a train. We talked in low voices of this and that, then suddenly Fritz took off his hat, seized my hand and kissed it before I could prevent him.

'Heaven doesn't always make the right men kings,' he said, trying to laugh.

Old Sapt's mouth twisted as he shook my hand.

'The devil,' said he, 'has his share in most things.'

The train came, and I got in. There were a few people around, and they looked curiously at us, as Sapt and Fritz, their hats in their hands, said goodbye. Perhaps they thought it was some great man travelling privately. They would have been disappointed if they had known that it was only I, Rudolf Rassendyll, a younger son of an English family. Yet, whatever I was now, I had been for three months a king. Perhaps I did not think so much of the experience because as the train moved away from Ruritania, I seemed to hear coming through the air into my ears and into my heart the cry of a woman's love – 'Rudolf! Rudolf! Rudolf!'

I can hear it now.

◆

The details of my return home can be of little interest. I went straight to the Alps, and spent a quiet ten days there. I sent a postcard to my brother Robert, telling him that I was soon coming back. I let my beard grow again.

When I got home, Rose was very annoyed that I had written no book, nor even collected any notes.

'We've wasted a lot of time trying to find you,' she said.

'I know,' I said. 'But why? I can take care of myself.'

'It wasn't that,' she answered. 'But I wanted to tell you about Sir Jacob Borrodaile. He's to be an ambassador, and is ready to take you with him.'

'Where is he going to?'

'To Strelsau. I believe it's a very nice place,' said Rose.

'I don't think I want to go,' I said with some determination.

'You might even become an ambassador yourself,' she urged.

'I don't want to become an ambassador.'

'It's more than you will ever be,' she said, annoyed at my refusal.

That is very likely true, but the idea of being an ambassador could hardly attract me. I had been a king!

Rose went away, and my brother Robert took out a magazine.

It had in it a photograph of the coronation at Strelsau. I sat silently looking at it.

'It's a strange likeness,' said my brother, looking at me curiously, and then looking at the picture of the King.

I said nothing, because though Robert is one of the best men in the world, and I would tell him any secret, this secret was not mine, so I could not tell it.

I have lived quietly since then. Once a year, though, I go to a small town this side of the Ruritanian border. There I meet Fritz, now happily married to the Countess Helga, and we spend a week together. I hear all the news of Strelsau, and often we talk of Sapt, the King, and of young Rupert. When the evenings come, we talk at last of Flavia, because every year Fritz brings me a red rose, and round it is a piece of paper with these words written on it:

'Rudolf – Flavia – always.'

I also send the same to her, the woman who is now the Queen of Ruritania and will always be the queen of my heart.

I still exercise myself with a sword, as somehow I have a feeling that I will meet young Rupert again and we will end the fight that was interrupted in the cool dark forest of Zenda.

Who knows?

ACTIVITIES

Chapters 1–3

Before you read

1 Read the Introduction and complete these statements.
  a Rudolf Rassendyll comes from ....
  b The imaginary country in which his adventures take place is called ....
  c Rudolf goes there to see the coronation of King ....
  d The new king and Rudolf Rassendyll both have .... hair.
  e The young Rudolf falls in love with ....

2 Find these adjectives in your dictionary. They are all in the story.
  earnest   fierce   merry
  Which adjective would you use to describe the following:
  a a wild animal
  b children at a birthday party
  c a hard-working but boring teacher
  d a group of friends at a pub
  e soldiers in battle
  f a poor quiet priest

3 Check the meanings of these titles in your dictionary. They tell us about a person's social or professional position.
  Chancellor   Colonel   Duke   Majesty   Marshal   sire
  a Which two titles refer to positions in the army or air force?
  b Which three titles refer to people with a royal position?
  c Which title is an important government position?

4 Find these words in your dictionary. They can all have a relationship with kings, queens and castles.
  bow   carriage   coronation   crown   drawbridge   moat   throne
  Write a sentence for each of the seven words. Use *king*, *queen* or *castle* in each of your sentences.

5 Find these words in your dictionary:

cellar   inch   lodge   rank   revolver   scorn (scornful/scornfully)

Complete this telephone conversation with the correct forms to the new words.

Policeman: Hello, Middlethorpe Police Station. Officer Rodgers speaking.

Duke: Officer, this is Duke Frederick. Please come quickly.

Policeman: Where are you now, sir?

Duke: I'm in the sitting-room of my ....

Policeman: And what is the problem?

Duke: I can hear noises below me in the .... I think there is a burglar in the house, just .... away from me.

Policeman: Are you alone?

Duke: Yes, I am, but I have a .... I'll shoot the burglar if I see him.

Policeman: Sir, it might be the wind or an animal. Don't do anything unreasonable.

Duke: Officer, what is your .... ?

Policeman: I'm just an ordinary policeman, sir, but I know my job.

Duke: I'm sure you do. I'm never .... of ordinary policemen.

Policeman Thank you, sir. I'm on my way.

After you read

6 Which of these are the same people?
   a The Duke of Strelsau
   b Rudolf Rassendyll
   c Black Michael
   d Princess Flavia
   e King Rudolf the Fifth
   f The brother of Rose's husband
   g The King's brother
   h The Duke of Strelsau's cousin
   i Black Michael's brother

7 Are these statements true or false? Correct the false ones.

  a Rudolf Rassendyll has led a useful life.

  b Rudolf travels from Paris on the same train as Princess Flavia.

  c Red hair is very common in Ruritania.

  d The Duke of Strelsau also wishes to be king.

  e The King is well known for his love of drink.

  f Rassendyll shaves off his beard.

  g Black Michael is surprised that the coronation takes place.

  h Michael knows that Rassendyll is not his brother.

8 Act out the conversation between Sapt and Rassendyll at the point where the former tries to persuade Rassendyll to take the place of the King at the coronation.

Chapters 4–6

Before you read

9 Do you think anyone in Ruritania will guess that Rassendyll is not the real king? Who and why?

10 What do you think Black Michael will do now?

11 Use your dictionary to check the meaning of the word *countess*. You are making a movie about a *countess*. Answer these questions about her.

  a Where does she live?

  b How many servants does she have? What do they do for her?

  c What kind of car does she own?

  d What kind of clothes does she wear?

  e What does she do on a typical weekend?

  f Which actress would you choose to play the role of the *countess*?

After you read

12 Who:

    a is killed protecting the King from Black Michael's men?

    b tells Black Michael about Rassendyll?

    c leaves a sword in a man's body?

    d are the three foreigners in the famous Six?

    e keeps Black Michael waiting?

    f does Fritz seem to be in love with?

    g writes the letter to Rassendyll?

    h escapes with the help of a table?

13 Originally Rassendyll was supposed to replace the King for the coronation only and then to leave Ruritania. Explain the circumstances that led to his change of plans.

Chapters 7–10

Before you read

14 Read the titles of Chapters 7–10 and answer the questions.

    A Question of Honour

    a Whose honour, do you think?

    Setting a Trap

    b Who do you think the trap is for?

    The Path to Heaven

    c What do you think the 'Path to Heaven' might be?

    A Dangerous Plan

    d What plan do you think Rassendyll and Sapt make?

    e Why is it dangerous?

After you read

15 Answer these questions.

 a How have Princess Flavia's feelings towards the King changed, and why?

 b What does Rassendyll tell Sapt he wants to do before he leaves Ruritania?

 c Who puts a knife into Rassendyll?

 d How is the real King guarded by the Duke's men in the old castle?

 e What is the 'Path to Heaven' and what is its purpose?

 f Why do the words of the Chief of the Strelsau Police worry Rassendyll?

 g What proposal does Rupert of Hentzau make to Rassendyll, and how does Rassendyll reply?

 h Who is the woman at the castle with the real King?

 i What does Rassendyll give to Flavia?

16 Rassendyll says that Michael '. . . probably thought that I was not acting for honour, but for myself.' What do you think?

17 Discuss the details of the plan to rescue the King.

Chapters 11–13

Before you read

18 How do you think the story will end for:

 a Black Michael?

 b Rudolf Rassendyll?

 c Princess Flavia?

 d King Rudolf?

 e Rupert of Hentzau?

After you read

19 Who:

    a has been promised to Rupert if he kills Rassendyll?

    b stops Detchard killing the real King?

    c helps Rassendyll in his fight with Detchard?

    d kills Michael?

    e jumps into the moat after the Duke has been killed?

    f finds Rassendyll just as Rupert is about to kill him?

    g faints on hearing that Rassendyll is not the King?

    h returns to a small town near the Ruritanian border every year?

20 Do you think it is really possible for one person to take the place of another without being discovered? Discuss the problems that would face someone trying to do this.

21 Take the parts of Rassendyll and Princess Flavia and act out the scene when she finds him in the forest, but without her fainting. Explain to each other what has happened and what you feel must happen in the future.

Writing

22 Rewrite the end of the story so that Rudolf Rassendyll becomes King of Ruritania and marries Princess Flavia.

23 Do you think Rassendyll would have made a better king than Rudolf the Fifth? Explain your reasons.

24 Write a newspaper report describing the coronation at Strelsau.

25 Discuss the importance of the idea of 'honour' in the book. How does it affect the events in the story?

26 Write a short information sheet about the (fictional) country of Ruritania at the time of the story. Include 'facts' about the cities, the countryside, the government and the lifestyles of the people.

27 What qualities do you feel have made *The Prisoner of Zenda* such a popular book?